How To Become a
Million Dollar Real Estate Agent In Your First Year

What Smart Agents Need To Know Explained Simply

By
Susan Smith Alvis

How To Become A Million Dollar Real Estate Agent In Your First Year: What Smart Agents Need To Know Explained Simply

Copyright © 2007 Atlantic Publishing Group, Inc.
1210 SW 23rd Place • Ocala, Florida 34474 • Phone 800-814-1132 • Fax 352-622-5836
Web site: www.atlantic-pub.com • E-mail: sales@atlantic-pub.com
SAN Number: 268-1250

ISBN-13: 978-1-60138-041-8 ISBN-10: 1-60138-041-0

Library of Congress Cataloging-in-Publication Data

Alvis, Susan Smith, 1969-
  How to become a million dollar real estate agent in your first year : what
smart agents need to know explained simply / Author: Susan Smith Alvis.
       p. cm.
  Includes bibliographical references and index.
  ISBN-13: 978-1-60138-041-8 (alk. paper)
  ISBN-10: 1-60138-41-0 (alk. paper)
  1. Real estate agents. 2. Real estate business. I. Title.

  HD1382.A55 2007
  333.33023'73--dc22
                              2006029747

EDITOR: Marie Lujanac • mlujanac817@yahoo.com

PROOFREADER: Angela C. Adams • angela.c.adams@hotmail.com

ART DIRECTION, FRONT COVER & INTERIOR DESIGN: Meg Buchner • megadesn@mchsi.com

GLOSSARY COMPILED BY: Christina Mohammed

Printed in the United States

Printed on Recycled Paper

Contents

Chapter 7 Becoming the Go-To Agent 99

Chapter 8 Selling Is Your Business— But Can You Sell? 109

Chapter 9 Making Plans for Success in Real Estate 125

Chapter 10 Referrals, Advertising, and Nonsense 137

Chapter 11
Becoming the Number One Agent in Your Area   151

Chapter 12 The Internet Agent   173

Chapter 13 Career and Family:
The Real Estate Balance   181

Appendix B

About The Author

Glossary: Terms New Agents Need to Know

Index

Foreword

As a multi-millionaire real estate investor and realtor®, I have realized two important facts about the real estate business. One: it is possible to make millions in real estate. Two: anyone can do it with the right knowledge and discipline. Susan Alvis in her book *How to Become a Million Dollar Real Estate Agent in Your First Year: What Smart Agents Need to Know* gives the reader the knowledge and teaches the necessary discipline to get there. As Susan Alvis says in Chapter One, you cannot be a successful real estate agent with the philosophy of a used car salesman. By that she means a real estate agent cannot just sit in his office and expect the business to come in. The agent needs to understand that the real estate profession is a career choice, but successful agents understand the business of real estate is also a lifestyle choice.

This is also a no-nonsense book that strips away the myths and glamour about the industry. As Susan Alvis points out, many new real estate agents believe that they will make big bucks easily in the profession. However, even a big producer who sells a million dollars worth of property may make only $42,000 a year, more or less, depending on the commission split with his or her broker. From that $42,000 a year, the agent will have to pay for his or her cost of business (as most agents work as independent contractors) including advertising, gas, car maintenance, dues, and fees. At the end of the year, a million dollar producer may net an income of less than $20,000, which is less than he or she can make flipping burgers. For new agents, selling a million dollars worth of property is something that they can only dream of. Often new agents struggle to get that first listing and it is most likely for a small $100,000 property. It is not surprising that the real estate profession has an extremely high turnover.

This book is not intended to discourage people from entering the industry but gives them the knowledge to do what is necessary to be successful in this business. Real estate is not for the weak-hearted or the lazy. It is a profession that requires hard work, creativity, flexibility, and a willingness to learn the business. Too often people who lack these qualities get discouraged and either drop out, or worse, lose their integrity. All agents in this industry need to be cognizant of ethics in each decision-making situation. Historically, real estate has been a cutthroat business where agents stoop to the most extreme levels to get a client and accordingly protect themselves. Such agents have given the real estate profession its questionable reputation and as a result, it has become highly regulated. Agents should not follow dishonest, underhanded practices for obvious reasons, but also because they are bad business practices in the long run and there is a strong likelihood agents will be penalized by the commission that regulates their local industry.

Susan Alvis also covers the issue of what the life of a real estate agent is like. Unlike other professions, where the person works 9 a.m. to 5 p.m., many real estate agents believe that they are on call 24 hours, 365 days a year. It is important for agents to recognize that family and time off are important to build a successful real estate business. Overworking leads to burnout and can be very damaging to one's family. It is important to recognize that no matter how urgent clients think the matter is, they will leave a message and wait until the morning or Monday to hear back from the agent if they encounter voice mail. I have never heard of a client terminating an agent because he did not take the client's call late at night or over the weekend. A timely reply to a client's call is important, but it can wait until a reasonable time.

Finally Susan Alvis provides a wealth of information on what an agent needs to know to be very successful in this industry. I encourage you to read this book. When you make your first million dollars, please remember to mail Susan Alvis a thank you letter or card. I am sure she will greatly appreciate it.

— Winston T. Rego

Winston T. Rego is a real estate investor in Greenville, South Carolina. He has doubled his own net worth and assets every year for the last four years and has grown his assets from five hundred thousand dollars in 2002 to over eight million dollars in 2006. Winston T. Rego is also a Commercial Realtor with Executive Choice Realty in Greenville, South Carolina and works exclusively with investors. Using ideas and techniques that he has developed to grow his own fortune, Mr. Rego assists his investor clients in acquiring and selling real estate to increase their cash flow and grow their net worth. Most of his clients see an annual return on investment in excess of 50 percent and many get returns in excess of 100 percent by investing in low risk, stable commercial real estate.

Winston can be contacted by e-mail at **WinstonRego@yahoo.com**.

Preface

I 'd like to thank all of the real estate agents who contributed to this book either directly or indirectly. Without you, this book would hold little meaning. Thank you for taking the time to contribute your knowledge and expertise on a field you know so well.

THANK YOU to everyone at Atlantic Publishing for making book number two a reality and for your support throughout the writing process of this book. To Angela Adams, a very special thank you for being a supportive editor and one I so much counted on for expertise and advice.

I also want to send a big THANK YOU to my extraordinary children Matthew and Amber for always tolerating me when I'm in front of the computer and to my husband Brent for being an excellent cook, THANK YOU for taking my place in the kitchen so I could write once more.

chapter one

So You Want To Be a Real Estate Agent

The Real Estate Myth

When you decided to become a real estate agent, you likely had a mental picture of what a real estate agent does, but you may have envisioned an agent who is just an agent and not necessarily a true professional in the business. Many people obtain their real estate license, hang it on the wall of a broker's office, and then just sit back and wait for clients. I call it the used-car-salesman-syndrome. They take their floor duty on occasion and they go on property tours to view the new office listings. Outside of these two great tasks, they do very little more. They seem to be perfectly content to hang out in the office of their broker while waiting for the phone to ring.

These agents do put in a great number of hours sitting around at their broker's office daydreaming of the sales they are going to make, but they have not ventured outside in the realm of actual sales work. Well, they can make a mean pot of coffee while they are waiting for their next client to show up.

Fifty-one percent of agents have a college degree, but the numbers of people who abandon the profession could be attributed to the lack of educational requirements to become an agent. It is often so easy to become a licensed real estate agent that some agents never take their job seriously. Real estate is not a nine-to-five job—it is a career choice, a lifestyle choice.

When you enter into real estate, you need to know that while you have a great opportunity to become successful, so did everyone else who dropped out of the profession before you. Sales trainers can show you what to do to be successful, but the truth is your success is entirely up to you. If you have looked at a home-based business or a direct selling opportunity in the past, you likely ended up on a mass marketing campaign for home-based businesses and if so, you are familiar with the following statement. "Be in business for yourself but not by yourself." What a nice thought. The reality is very different in real estate. In the business of commissions earned on secured and closed sales, you are in business for yourself and you are most definitely by yourself. Sure, a broker and all of his top producing agents will tell you something very similar to the above statement but ultimately, it comes down to you and what you are capable of doing in your business.

Sales coaches, brokers, other agents, and top producers can show you what to do; authors can write about it; but when it gets down to business your business depends on you to make it a success. What you do now will help determine how successful you are in the future. Your broker has a vested interest in seeing you succeed but most brokers are listing and selling property, too. Your broker has absolutely no financial advantage in helping you for an unlimited time because you cut into their bottom line. Few brokers want a liability taking up space in their office. It is up to you to get out there in the community and start working your business. You have to be self-inspired and you need to be able to motivate yourself while networking in all of the right places.

A big misconception a new agent may have is that there is an endless flow of customers who bring their business to you. Many seasoned realtors are likely smirking right now because they have observed others who were similarly delusional.

Real estate is a difficult business to break into successfully and only the hard-working, dedicated professionals ever make it. Many agents will keep their license active, sell a few houses a year and claim to be full-time in a business, and only a few will reach million dollar agent status. To be a successful real estate agent, you will need to sell MILLIONS. One million dollars in agent sales only adds up to about $42,000 a year. Depending on your agent split with your broker, it may be slightly higher or it could be considerably lower and hardly considered a lucrative income.

For you to understand how much effort goes into selling a million dollars worth of property, you need to consider the following: if you sell 10 houses at $100,000 each, you will have sold one million dollars in real estate. In some areas, this is an easy task, but in rural or depressed areas sales may be difficult. Too many agents for a smaller market, rising interest rates, much lower home prices, and many other factors can prevent sales from mounting toward the million dollar mark. A poor market can be discouraging for new agents, but there is a positive side. Consider agents who sell properties on waterfronts. They can often sell one home at a million dollars or several million dollars, making it relatively easy for an agent to reach million dollar status overnight.

Depending on your area and the market where you work, you will quickly know how many homes or properties you will need to sell each year to reach million dollar agent status. Again, in some areas, one may just do the trick. In other areas, it may be a struggle to find one property over $100,000.

A high turnover in the business is the result of myths and misconceptions that leave the agent bewildered and broke, but those agents who recognize the profession as a true career opportunity find there is simply no better way to make a living. These individuals know they have to work hard for every sale they get in a business where agents quickly understand the meaning of "cutthroat."

Real estate is not for the weak-hearted. Be thick-skinned to survive because there is always someone who wants your business and your clients. In fact, many agents pull off some pretty hysterical, unethical tactics to gain your business. One of my best friends in a real estate office where I worked showed me what a fine line friendship and business truly can be. It was a lesson I will be eternally grateful for even though I have no respect for him now.

You have to remember, when it comes to large amounts of money, anyone will stab you in the back for your commission unless you are working with family. (Even then, some agents have to watch their back!) You will have to decide what you are willing to do for a sale, but if you are in the business to stay, ethical practices will serve you well.

One reason the suggestions in the following chapters will work is because you are going to open up possibilities working outside your so called "circle of influence." You will develop a circle of contacts instead and these people may not even know you personally. Believe me when I tell you, most agents find the majority of their sales do not come from personal friends and family. In fact, you may end up very shocked to learn your cousin, your best friend, and even your hairdresser will not buy from you. Maybe they want to keep their financial situation from you, or perhaps they just do not want you to earn a commission from them. For whatever reason, they will take their business somewhere else, and you will feel betrayed, but if you are looking out for your future, you will see plenty of opportunities for sales.

In this book, we are going to cover the basics of becoming not just a good agent, but one of the best agents your area has ever known. You will see why ethical practices will put you at the forefront of your business sooner than ruthless principles. If you practice what you learn, you will be rewarded with the income you desire.

Wise real estate agents will not steal business or take unethical steps to have a good income. They earn their business and once they have it, they keep it for the lifetime of the client. You may lose one or two along the way, but the business you gain will be yours. After you learn how to ensure client loyalty, you will have clients for the life of your career. Neither will you have to depend on your circle of influence because your career will be set, using the methods we are going to discuss.

What Is a Real Estate Agent?

Once you earn your real estate license, your primary goal is and always will be to bring a buyer and seller together regardless of which one you represent. You get paid only after the transaction reaches the closing table.

As you deal with your clients, you can write many offers to purchase, but unless you can write winning offers to purchase, you cannot earn money. Further, just because you write an offer to purchase, the contract may not be accepted and if not, you will not get paid. Finally, even with an accepted offer to purchase, if the deal does not close, you do not get paid. So let us find out how to get paid.

Agents are their own bosses. They are independent contractors, meaning they are directly responsible for their own income. They must work with buyers and sellers to generate sales. First, they must obtain listings of potential sales; then they must move buyers in the direction of writing a successful offer to purchase. In other words, earn it, and the commission checks will be written in your name. Ten percent of real estate agents do 90 percent of the business. Let us delve into a realistic job description of a licensed agent.

Agent Characteristics and Tasks

- They are **active listeners**.

- They are **educated on all aspects of real estate transactions** such as showing property, writing and presenting contracts, negotiating offers to purchase and securing a sale.

- **Good real estate agents know how to gain new business**. They place new-home flyers and ads, they call prospective clients on the phone, and they canvass areas for new business. In general, they work long days drumming up new business regardless of how much current business they have.

- **Agents often line up other professionals** such as termite inspections, home inspections, and appraisals.

- **On land deals, agents stay in close contact with the surveying company** so that the property is surveyed promptly.

- **Winning agents have the ability to sell using sales techniques** to bring buyers and sellers together in a timely fashion.

- **Agents learn to master the Internet effectively**, and they are able to drive traffic to their Web site.

- **Agents list properties that are marketable** and work with buyers who are pre-qualified and ready to buy.

- **They take floor calls in their broker's office.**

Agents Responsibilities

- **They are babysitters** when showing a couple a new home and often feel as though they are running a day care road show as they take families through one home after another.

- **They are marriage counselors** when one part of the happy couple has been less than honest about the couple's state of financial affairs.

- **They are master negotiators** when there appears to be no part of the deal left to negotiate. Determined never to say die, hard-hitting sales people know how to push a deal forward.

- **Agents are financial advisors** even when they do not want to be.

- **They are parents** when a young person needs advice, without overstepping boundaries of professionalism.

- **They are a friend** to the client who clearly needs one.

- **They are reliable business partners** in a real estate transaction, remaining professional at all times.

- **They can even be a client's guardian or protector.** In many cases agents even have to become the client's power of attorney.

Did you realize you were going to wear so many different hats in your new career? You will become very successful in the real estate business because you will be your client's best friend from the beginning until the end of their real estate transaction. People buy from people they like. After all, would you buy from someone you would not consider a friend? Absolutely not! This is why wearing the professional multi-tasking hat will prove to be beneficial in your career as a real estate agent. If you can become agile, you will be more likeable because your style and work ethics will appeal to a larger number of clients. You are not only going to be your clients' advisor and agent but you will become their professional friend.

Who Are These People Called Real Estate Agents?

Many people believe agents are overpaid for what they do. In fact, some people balk at the thought of paying agents because they believe as homeowners; they know more about their property than any real estate agent would ever know. And they are right. However, even though a homeowner knows his or her home best, his efforts are not likely to sell the property. Owners are emotionally and financially attached to their homes and as a real estate professional, you will not be. They will expect clients to appreciate certain points about the property just as they do. Even if you like your clients, you will never see their property through their eyes even though you can try.

Understand that homeowners want you to see what they see in the property. They want to believe an agent has a vested interest in selling the property and genuinely sees its worth, although meeting their expectations can be a challenge. Still, a homeowner will need you to care about their property and whether it can be sold for the amount they need to realize financially. Otherwise, they really will not appreciate your efforts.

Agents are licensed real estate professionals and what makes agents a needed force within the community is the fact they know their business as any true professional should. Agents are supposed to be educated on staging homes, comparative market analysis, and the overall real estate market. If you are going to be considered an agent worth using in your local area, you need to be professional and knowledgeable in all aspects of real estate.

What Do Real Estate Agents Earn?

Even if you talk with some of the more seasoned real estate agents, you will find earnings can and will vary. The best agents in the world know they are not only as good as their last sale but that their last sale can truly be their last sale. With this in mind, real estate agents know they can earn income only if they are working toward the common goal of bringing buyers and sellers together. This means it will be to your advantage as a new real estate agent to write winning offers the first time out with your buyers so sellers will be able to accept them.

Unless you are an agent/assistant working for or with a top producer, chances are you will be working on commission only. If you are going to be working with a top producer as their assistant, you need to break away on your own quickly because you will never be able to realize the million dollar agent status as an assistant.

A new agent cannot determine their first year's earnings in real estate. There are many factors to take into consideration. Understand there is money in real estate and someone is going to make it regardless of what market you are in and regardless of how many agents are in your area. The best I can offer is to tell you to plan to make much money and then do not disappoint yourself. Go out there and make it.

A Day in the Life of a Real Estate Agent

It is costly to become a real estate agent and even more expensive to remain one, so in choosing this career you should be prepared to work, and if not, you will still be required to pay dues.

Real estate agents have thrown numbers around within my hearing for a great number of years regarding their expenses: like, "I spent $5,000 last year entertaining clients" or "My dues took all of my commission." While this seems like an unlikely scenario, it is your reality if you remain on your sitter-downer rather than starting from day one working your business. Dues for real estate agents are expensive, and a good number of agents spend too much entertaining clients.

It is expected that you spend your gas money showing clients' houses and interesting property whether you drive them around or they follow you from property to property. It is also expected that you to treat them to lunch or maybe even a latte if you are going to be out all day or one afternoon full of house hunting. However, find your favorite spot for budget meals and avoid taking your clients out to the most expensive spot in town. They did not buy from you yet! A stop at Subway for sandwiches where you can afford the tab is just as acceptable as a dinner at Outback Steakhouse. An agent I know used to say to me, "Susan, do not treat them to the steak. They will think you can afford the steak. Treat them to a burger and they will appreciate it." Who knows if this holds any psychological meaning or not but I fed clients burgers, pizza, and, yes, occasionally steak. However, my investments in steak did not pay off any faster than other sales!

An average real estate agent depends on referrals and the calls they receive through taking "floor duty" in their broker's office. Neither source of income should be used as a security blanket. Usually a broker who assigns floor duty to their agents posts a calendar and assigns each agent a pre-set number of days per month with designated hours to be in the office. When you are on "floor duty" you will answer incoming calls and visit with walk-in guests or clients. This is a great opportunity to gain listings and to speak with prospective buyers. A newbie should always take floor duty and also try to pick up any extra floor shifts when time permits. In large offices, this is never a problem because someone is always trying to get rid of floor duty at the last minute.

One of the first real estate offices where I worked had a large number of agents and listings so I had the opportunity to take floor time anytime I wanted it because I stayed in my office as much as possible. Doing so enabled me to volunteer for other agents' floor time if they were going out for an extended lunch or if they had a walk-in who wanted to be shown a listing immediately. I considered myself their back-up if they were called away from floor time. All agents recognized the importance of new contacts so there were many top agents who hung their license at this firm and used the broker's numerous listings to help them gain contacts. Still, none of the top agents relied on floor time to carry them. They knew they had to work outside the office to gain new business.

Floor duty is just one way to gain business, but there are so many other things you can do to find sales and listings that will ultimately increase your bottom line. Following are things you can do that will yield positive results if done consistently. Later we will explore them, but for now look at what a successful real estate agent does in a work day.

- **They call new for-sale-by-owner homes listed** in all of the local papers each morning or each afternoon.

- **They take any floor duty opportunities offered** and pick up any additional floor time even if only for an hour so that another agent can go to lunch.

- **Agents who canvass for business do so daily or on a set schedule**. Some agents even go door to door when they canvass.

- **They plan open houses and send out invitations.**

- **When working with buyers, each day the real estate agent should be checking the multiple listing service** for new listings which might meet the needs of the buyer.

- **When working with buyers, if unable to find the right**

property, agents will drive around the area and find something—even if it means knocking on doors!

- **They spend a certain amount of time each day planning advertising and marketing.** However, they spend very little time on this and do it only to ensure they think before acting on the numerous advertising opportunities presented to them.

- **Each morning they fax any new listings to every office in their area** and take the time to send out a listing sheet by mail to all of the top agents or offices in the area.

- **Good agents know it is important to stay on top of all real estate transactions until the deal is closed.** They will take the time to line up any home inspectors and all the other professionals needed to complete a deal. In the case of a cash-at-closing deal, agents will line up the appraiser for the property, ensure a title search is done, and will be ready before the closing.

- **Once a week only, the agent will take time to meet with mortgage brokers** who are trying to gain their business It is important to get to know the lenders and their loan officers so good agents make time for them at least once a week. As business picks up, these appointments may occur a couple of times a month, but top agents remain connected to the lenders in their area.

- **Million dollar agents cold call.** Yes, cold call. It is not a misprint. Successful agents know they need to be aggressive on their climb to the top and once they get to the top they know cold calling may be necessary to ensure they stay there.

- **Every day, the agent places flyers and business cards wherever they go** and several times a week they go out specifically to place cards.

- **Once a day, dedicated agents will check on their Web presence** and do what they can to improve it. They also make routine updates on their Web site and check their e-mail daily.

- **A good agent will work the expired listings** and they will work the listings that are just pulled from the market.

- **They work on their upcoming promotion** which we will discuss later.

As you can see from the list above, an agent has plenty to do throughout the day. In fact, if you ever hear a real estate agent say they have nothing to do, remember this to-do list. Every agent in the business will always have something to do, and new agents have plenty to do as they begin to build their business!

Hours and Income—You Get to Decide

What a way to make a living. As a real estate agent, you get to decide when you work, how long you work, what you do when you work, and ultimately, you get to write your own paycheck. Can it get much better! Real estate agents, as self-employed individuals, gain many perks by being an independent contractor. For instance, they can leave work in the middle of the day to go to their child's school play. They can take off a day if they need dental work and best of all, there is no PTO time used because PTO in real estate means paid-time-on! While sometimes agents will miss the fringe benefits of working for a more traditional employer such as health insurance and the coveted paid time off, take a look at what a real estate agent can realize in their chosen career:

- **An above average income** with the possibility of earning a six-figure income

- **Extended vacations** anytime of the year with no one to approve or deny your vacation request

- **The ability** to be your own boss

- **The flexibility** in scheduling

- **The ability** to work from almost anywhere as long as he or she has a laptop and cell phone available

- **Endless opportunities** to acquire real estate

- **An opportunity to see more**, do more, and be more than he or she ever thought possible with or without a college degree

With all of these fringe benefits, why do you think so many agents are overworked? It usually boils down to three or four reasons. The agent did not plan, did not work their plan if they had one, did not set goals, and finally and most important, they did not set office hours. One thing we are going to discuss is how to manage your time wisely, but realize that goal setting is important, time management is crucial, and working productively is mandatory for your success.

Real estate agents are able to spend minimal time learning their trade. After they complete licensing requirements for the state where they will be practicing real estate, they can start a profitable career with income which can reach the level of life-changing. A prominent real estate firm, Keller Williams, proposes a realistic goal. Their company goal is to develop 8,200 millionaires. Their mission statement states clearly what they are trying to achieve. They aspire to "build careers worth having, businesses worth owning, and lives worth living."

Real estate is a career worth having if you choose to be exceptional be willing to do what others will not do—to have a career and business worth having and live a rewarding life thanks to the business that you successfully built.

You have chosen to try a new career. Now, it is up to you to make sure you make it a career worthy of your time. The only way to do this is to jump right in and get busy building a business you can be very proud to call your own.

The following case study is from Ben Smith, a real estate agent in Johnson City, Tennessee. He knows what it takes for a new agent to succeed in real estate and he offers these tips.

Ben Smith

There are several keys to becoming a successful realtor in your first year on the job. It is important to get your name out to as many people as possible. It is a good idea to do a mail out to friends, family members, fellow church members, and people in the community announcing that you have started a career in real estate. This will let people know that you are now practicing real estate and can help them with any needs they may have.

Another key to getting a quick start is to take as much floor time in the office as possible to allow you to answer cold call, get new prospects, learn the office's listings, and have the opportunity to get buyer and seller leads. You may also want to speak to some of the top agents in the office and offer your services for clients they may not have time for. In turn you can offer them a referral fee. This will help you learn the secrets of the trade from an established realtor and also pick up some clients you would not otherwise have.

As a new realtor it is challenging to get listings, so you should work the For Sale By Owners. I have the most success by going to speak with the sellers in person. A good way to get your foot in the door with FSBOs is to offer them free services, such as letting them borrow "open house" signs, offering tips for staging their home for showings, and answering any general questions they may have to help you build a relationship. They will be familiar with you if they decide to list their property. More than 80 percent of FSBOs end up listing with a real estate agent, so that is a good way to get listings.

Another way to get your name seen in public is to wear your company name badge wherever you go and always carry business cards with you. Often you will overhear someone in a grocery store, restaurant, and other places talking about homes, and this is the ideal time to introduce yourself and hand them a business card. The key is to keep your eyes and ears open because you never know where you will find your next client. Finally the most important thing is to set goals for yourself and work, work, work to achieve your goals. There is always another agent out there working harder, so the key is to out-work your competition.

Ben Smith • 423-677-9304
www.tricityareaproperties.com

IMPORTANT TIPS from chapter one

1. You are in this business by and for yourself.

2. Work your business or you will find yourself out of business.

3. A million dollars in sales earns you a mediocre income. Several million dollars in sales can change your life significantly.

4. Developing a circle of good contacts is better than any circle of influence.

5. There is no reason for a new agent to have an astronomical entertainment bill at the end of the year, and if you watch what you spend you will not have unnecessary expenses.

6. Goal-setting is important.

7. Time-management is crucial.

8. Working productively is mandatory if you are going to be successful.

9. PTO time means PAID TIME ON!

chapter two

Ethical Agent Practices

In real estate dealings, you will meet some of the most wonderful people in the world. You will also deal with the shrewdest men and women who will smile and pat you on the back on their way out to meet your clients for lunch. It is the nature of the business. However, do not be too hard on the agents who practice this behavior. It is not just the business of real estate; this is common practice anytime money is involved, but you do not have to conduct your business greedily. In fact, if you conduct your business with a smidgen of ethics, you will likely stand out in a crowd when it is most important.

Real estate is a funny business anyway. Clients who are my clients this week could be your clients next week and vice-versa because many people have no concept of loyalty when it comes to a client-agent relationship. When you are fortunate enough to find a loyal client, treasure them because they will be the people who will send you referrals and will remember you whenever they need a real estate agent again.

In sales jobs where large commissions are at stake, it is hard to trust anyone. Even agents in your own office will woo your client when there is enough money on the table. If you are honest with yourself, you may find you are even tempted. Do not give in to the root of all evil; keep your business dealings honest and straightforward, and believe me when I tell you, money will come your way.

What Kind of Agent Do You Want to Be?

When you enter any career, you have a unique opportunity for a better start. Normally, a job or career change will open a door to new possibilities that can enable you a fresh start should you need or want one. Regardless of what you have done in the past or how you have conducted previous business, I urge you to start your real estate business on the right foot. Hop along on the right one through your career because people want to do business with people they can trust rather than the good ol' boys where a handshake does not mean what it used to.

For a new agent, setting your standards from the beginning of your new career can be as important as goal setting. There are a number of things you will never want to become involved in while you are a licensed real estate agent. Several things come to mind, but for now, remember three things. First, always disclose the truth to your client. Second, always put your client's needs first and, finally, never lie to a client to make a sale. Someone could write a book on a list of things you need to avoid but for the most part, you need to set your own standards and abide by them at all costs. If you are ever placed in a potentially compromising situation with a client, do yourself a favor and walk away.

Following are some tips and guidelines to keep in mind.

- **Always treat others as you want to be treated** and never give more consideration to one client over another. Everyone is equal and while a commission on a $500,000 house is fabulous, you will likely gain more referral business from the person buying a $60,000 home who is treated as if they are buying a $500,000 home. It is important to remember the people who are buying high-end homes often do not notice exceptional customer service because they are accustomed to getting it. However, those who seldom make big purchases are likely to remember the names of people who gave them the royal treatment.

- **People want to be told the truth.** It may cost you one sale but it will likely earn you many others. If you are working with a client, it is your obligation to disclose anything you know to be wrong with the property and if you do not disclose it, it could prove to be a costly mistake. Always disclose everything you know about the property to your buyer as a buyer's agent and always be forthcoming with your sellers. There is no substitute for honest business dealings.

- **Buyers and sellers today are more knowledgeable** about real estate than ever before. With the Internet educating people on all aspects of a real estate transaction, the days of bluffing your way through a question and answer session are over. As a real estate professional, you must know what you are talking about if you are going to be successful. If you are someone who must really study before it sinks in, accumulate all the information you can on your trade and get busy studying your business. Whatever it takes, know your trade.

- **As a real estate agent, you have a fiduciary duty to your client.** This goes beyond simply showing your client a property and sprinting to the closing table. What this means is you are expected to conduct your business within the circle of the highest moral standards and ethical principles. Confidentiality is a must and clients deserve the opportunity to work with an upstanding member of the real estate community. If you cannot uphold your fiduciary duty, you will not last very long in this business. Legally, you are expected to perform within the confines of client-agent relationship, and if you cannot do this you have no business in the real estate business.

- **Just so you know, as a real estate agent, there will be times when your buyer will not buy unless you pressure them into buying.** However, there comes a time when the way you do this would be considered unethical. If you can only sell by telling some sort of tale such as "I know for a fact there is another offer coming in on the home," you will eventually have a rude awakening. Someone will call up the listing agent and ask if you told them the truth and you will then lose a client and a deal.

I want you to see what it is you can do to keep yourself out of the clutches of unethical practices. Understandably, you will have to do hard selling to close enough deals to place you among the ranks of the top agents in your area. Learn what to avoid and what you can do to ethically to close each of your real estate transactions successfully, and you will be glad you did.

Margie Larkins

"More people are buying average-priced homes than high-priced homes. It is important to be just as happy selling a $50,000 house as anything else because your client will send you many referrals if you work hard for them. One of the first clients I had in the business bought a house for around $15,000. She paid cash for the house and later referred her brother to me when he moved home after military duty. He bought a home which cost more than his sister's purchase, and both clients sent business my way. See, it pays to be happy working with clients from all economic backgrounds."

margielarkins@realtor.com

"We Specialize in Personalized Service"
Serving East Tennessee for more than 30 Years
423-246-5700

How to Treat Your Clients

As a new agent, you need to decide how you want to conduct your day-to-day business and how to handle your clients. If you want to be successful, you can be; but in sales, it does not happen unless you incorporate the golden rule and treat others as you wish to be treated.

In addition to treating your clients with respect, you must decide how much time you are going to spend with a client and how much access your clients will have to you. Many clients will not care about your time with your family—only your availability to them.

When I was in real estate, my business card listed my cell phone number, my home phone number, the office number, and even my pager number. Would you like to know how quickly I regretted this? Fast! While you must be available to your clients, you will need to spend more time being productive and less time cleaning up messes. Later we will discuss achieving the perfect balance, but for now, take a look at how easy it is to develop an ethical, trustworthy relationship with your client. It is so simple.

- **Do what you say you are going to do** when you say you are going to do it.

- **Always** return phone calls.

- **Never** make up an answer — find out the real one.

- **Be honest and direct** with your client.

- **Keep your client** relationships professional.

My mom is the only person I know who can turn a client into a genuine life-long friend. While I like to have friends, she *loves* to have friends and enjoys having people around her all of the time. However, thanks to ten-plus years in the real estate business, she is likely to run out of hours in a day soon. She is one of the few realtors I know who will not only sell someone a house but will literally run errands for them during the entire transaction. She has the patience to do it. I do not and most people do not. Many people would do what she does for the income it allows her. Her clients become her friends and they send their friends to her and so on. However, she never enjoys time to herself and the truth is, while her income is better than the average real estate agent's income, many would not feel the time lost with family would be worth it.

It is great to befriend a client but one thing to bear in mind is this can often become a way for people to tie up your time. As a million dollar real estate agent, you want to have friendly relationships, but you never want to become a taxi-driver moving quickly from home to home just so the client can "get an idea of what they may want." If you become friendly with clients, meeting for drinks after work and having luncheons at the country club, do not be surprised if the client begins to show no sign of urgency in finding a new home or investment property. After all, why should they? They are having a great time running around with a new buddy!

Ethical Issues

Most Boards of Realtors have an advisory board in place for disciplinary actions for agents who are unable to conform to acceptable and ethical practices. This board is in place to ensure buyers and sellers are protected from the undesirables of the business. Normally, agents are not brought up on charges for theft or other unsavory business practices but it does happen. Agents are people and not everyone in the business will follow ethical practices. Still, you must try your best to protect yourself, starting with making good decisions and thinking ahead. Remember when you are showing property to stay with your clients at all times when you are walking them through a home. Do not turn them loose in someone else's home. If you do and things are missing later when the seller returns, it will be your fault.

It is also important for you to advise your home sellers about ethical issues and let them know that they should take all precautionary measures to ensure they protect their valuables and their medications. Encourage your clients never to leave anything such as money, jewelry, or prescription medications in plain view. In other words, just do not tempt a potential thief.

You never know who will be viewing the house and it is not fair to your client to assume everyone who goes through the property will be aboveboard.

Common pitfalls can be avoided if you take measures to ensure you have pre-qualified your clients while making sure you never leave a client in a home unattended. Even in new constructions, occasionally tools and things have been left behind so stay with your clients and avoid problems later.

Another thing you may want to consider is the fact that if you conduct your business ethically, should a rare mishap occur, you will be cleared of any wrongdoing if clients in the past have found you to be honest in all other practices. This is just one more reason to stay with your clients and to conduct your business with professionalism at the center focus of your business.

Things to Remember Ethically and Morally

As you begin your career in real estate, you may be looking for ways to occupy your free time, and we covered some great ways to do this in the last chapter. While there is nothing wrong with the occasional lunch out with a client, there is always a point where you can set yourself up for failure in this business. Let me put it into perspective for you and I will try not to sound like a fuddy-duddy. Having a great time is wonderful. In fact, I used to be an advocate for having a good time but a good time in business can cost you your livelihood. In real estate, there are many opportunities to run around in the little inner circles and there are more party crowds than you can count in a business full of fun-loving people. Many people get into this business for the party, and it can consume a person. Take it from me, keep it professional from the beginning and you will keep your professional image intact while making more money than you ever thought possible.

Other tips to remember:

- **Be a listener and not a talker**. What you learn from your clients should stay between you and your clients. However, if you have a client who becomes your friend and they begin to tell you things you would be better off not knowing, make a judgment call and cut the conversation off before it starts. You would be surprised what a client will tell their real estate agent and if you cannot stop a client from telling you things you do not want to know, you would be better off to let them find another real estate agent. Remember a chatty client cuts into your bottom line. Heartless? Maybe so, but very true. You are a real estate agent and not your client's hair dresser or psychologist. Just try to keep your mind on the money while ensuring your client's needs are met as well.

- **A good practice to follow in this business** is never to get into the habit of going into meetings with the banker and your client if it can be helped. This is not always possible and sometimes, it cannot be avoided. However, many of your wealthier clients probably prefer the time alone with their lender and you never want to be privy to information which could eventually seep out through the banking industry or any other way. Do not be naïve and believe bankers never talk to anyone. I know from experience they do and I do not want you to catch the blame because you know what your client looks like on paper. I could always pre-qualify my clients and then easily turn them over to the lender without being present for all of the particulars of their credit and financial history. However, many real estate agents sit with their clients when the client requests that they do. View this meeting as none of your business and a waste of productive time and find a way to skip out when your client sits down with their loan officer. Let the lenders be lenders and you be the real estate professional focused on the transaction of bringing buyer and seller together.

- **When a buyer insists** you know all about their finances, do remember your legal fiduciary duty and keep all confidences.

- **Always put the interests of your client first**, and the sales will follow. Agents who become too interested in the sale itself and cannot make the time to be interested in the client's wants and needs will not go far in this people-oriented business. Remember, you need your clients to believe you are *genuinely* interested in helping them and the only way to do this is to be *genuinely interested* in helping them!

- **Use strong ethical business practices** in all areas of your business. Be the kind of agent who is as good as his word and handshake. There is enough business to go around without underhanded tactics. However, be ready to play hardball with the agents who use these practices. Do not just lie down and play dead!

Build your business on a strong foundation, and you will be a real estate agent who will be able to stand on reputation alone.

Ben Smith

The most important part of becoming a successful real estate agent is to be honest and treat others as you would want to be treated. If you live by this rule you might lose a sale or two, but for every sale you lose you will gain ten. By treating people the right way you will get tons of referrals and also build a good name in the process.

Ben Smith
423-677-9304
www.tricityareaproperties.com

IMPORTANT TIPS from chapter two

1. Remember the golden rule, and it will carry you as far as any other piece of advice.

2. Keep client relationships professional.

3. Be as good as your word and do what you say you are going to do.

4. Never "wing it." Find out real answers to real questions.

5. Return phone calls.

6. Remember your fiduciary duty to your clients.

7. Treat all clients equally regardless of how wide their purse strings are.

8. Spend your time being productive and you will spend less time cleaning up messes.

9. Your job is to bring buyers and sellers together and a lender's job is to bring buyers and money together.

10. Put your clients first and give them the royal treatment as long as they are your client.

chapter three

Company Matters

Once you get your real estate license, you will face one of the most difficult decisions of your career. You will need to decide where you want to hang your license. Naturally, you will want to set up appointments with several offices so you can check out the office close-up and personal and the broker can interview you. There are some things to consider when you begin to contemplate where you would like to work. Following are some items to keep in mind when you begin your search for the perfect real estate office.

Choosing a Real Estate Office

When you set off to find the real estate office of your dreams, know it will not be an easy task to locate the perfect office. Concentrate on the things most important to you and then try to locate an office which will meet your needs.

It is very possible to make the same amount of money regardless of where you are affiliated if you are doing most of the work yourself and not just sitting around waiting for the phone to ring.

Any broker would be honored to have a self-starting agent so where you choose to work should rely on the main driving force of this business—money. When it comes down to it, your agent-broker split will be the single most important factor weighing on your decision.

Which Office Will Be Right for You?

Before you make your office appointments to tour the area brokers' offices and meet with the managing brokers, take into consideration some of these important factors.

- How close is the office to your home?

- Does the real estate office have a good mix of listings—residential, commercial, and acreage?

- Does the office have a property management department and is it handled with office agents?

- Does the office have a relocation department and how are they handled within the office?

- Are private offices available or do you share a cubicle? What is your work space like and how important is it to you?

- Take an office tour and find out how the other agents like working with the broker and other agents in the office.

- How much does the broker charge for company advertising and what fees will you have beyond your MLS dues and other fees?

- What is the broker/agent split? Is the split offered on a graduated scale?

- How much sales volume does the firm realize each year?

- How does the community view this real estate firm? If you do not know, get out and ask. Go to area businesses and ask them for a real estate referral or pick up the phone and call around to conduct a survey and tell the business owners why you want to know. Work for an office with a good reputation and work for a broker people recognize.

Remember when you start your search for a real estate office you are going to have as much to offer a real estate firm as they will have to offer you. If you are career-minded and plan to do everything you can to make it to the top of your profession, express this to the brokers you meet. When I was in real estate, I worked in several offices and the only time I ever moved was because of a better split or opportunity with one exception. I have worked on a 60/40 split, 50/50 (which is a joke, by the way), and an 80/20 split.

If you think a split is not a big deal, consider this: if you make $100,000, your income is $80,000 on an 80/20 split and do I need to tell you what it is on the 50/50 split that many brokers tend to give new agents? I always looked at it this way: I do not like anyone well enough to give them $20,000 or $30,000. A savvy broker will tell you all sorts of good stuff to convince you to work with them on this split, but do not buy into it. They need you worse than you need them if you are a producer and you, my friend, are going to produce!

In the defense of many successful brokers, you cannot blame a broker for trying to get their agents to work for them for a little bit of nothing, which is what I call a 50/50 split. Still, when it comes down to negotiating splits which do not sound that great ask the broker what they will be doing for you and find out why they think the split arrangement is a good deal. Once they explain it, you will want to consider all your options. After all, there will be many offices for you to examine and you need to know what each broker plans to do for you because you know what you will be doing for them and that is making them money!

Another thing to watch for when you step into the negotiation of an agent/broker split is what is known as an advertising fee. Many brokers will charge their agents an advertising fee. This is the fee which helps with the office costs as much as homes magazines, office signs, and other things the broker provides. Be careful though. You should never pay more than 5 percent toward ads because a good managing broker can manage their portion of the split to take care of these things. Besides, most agents pay for their own property signs as well as open house signs (and directional signs). Many agents pay for their own advertising as well so I hesitate to even mention a 5 percent advertising fee. In some cases, the advertising fee is taken straight off the top of the commission and is just another way for the broker to realize more of your income so you need to know what the fee will pay for on your behalf.

Remember whom you are working for (yourself) when you sit down with a broker and what your income goals are for your business. Basically, a commission structure is usually based on 5 percent for new construction, 6 percent for residential, and 10 percent on commercial property or vacant land. The percent can vary by area, but this is the normal commission structure in the United States. Here is how this breaks down. For example, you sell a home for $250,000. The total commission due to the agents is $15,000, based on a 6 percent commission. However, you sold the home and did not list it so $7,500 goes to the listing office and $7,500 to the selling agent's office. You are working on a 60/40 split so you end up with $4,500 and your broker takes in $3,000. Of course, if you were working on an 80/20 split, you would have ended up with $6,000 and the broker would have profited $1,500. Not a bad split for the broker. Do you see why I am not an advocate of the so-called advertising fee?

Consider the same scenario with an agent advertising fee attached. Most of the time these fees are attached on a higher split ratio than a 60/40, but the 60/40 split means that you sold the $250,000 home and your office takes in the $7,500. Immediately, a 5 percent advertising fee comes off the top of the $7,500 which is $375, leaving $7,125 on the table. You take home $4,275 on the 60/40 split and your broker gets $2,850. However, that is really not the case because they also get the $375 for advertising so basically they took home $3,225 and you took home $4,275. See how this advertising fee works? When it gets right down to it, you are working on a 57/43 split in this case scenario.

Some of the most ridiculous agent splits are in offices with many agents. The broker will have this fabulous reputation for being good to their agents and in truth; they probably are. Still, they offer their agents an insulting split and tell them it is because the agents are working for one of the best companies in the area. However, if these agents would think a little more of their own incomes than the income of the broker and insist on a fair split for everyone, they would see how quickly the broker would initiate a pay raise instead of risk losing agents and listings.

There are many other factors to consider when choosing a real estate office, but as a new agent you should find the agent-broker split one of the most important factors if you are shopping for a home office where you would like to establish your career. Remember, some brokers will try to sell you on the fact that it can be expensive to help an agent get started. When they talk to you about an agent split, they will often let you in on all of the expenses they incur with new agents. Save the broker and yourself time and let the broker know up front that you are looking for an office that will cut you a good split and let them know you are all about the money. After all, they will talk a mean talk about money too so why not just lay all the cards on the table and tell them you are money-driven and career-minded. You will not be an agent any broker will need to very much money on because you will be out in the field working your own business.

As an established agent, you will probably have a following once you have been in the business for some time. For future reference, should the need present itself for you to move offices, make sure you take the time to mention how many listings you have to a new broker. If you have a track record in any sales-oriented career, whether it is in real estate or through any other sales background, make sure you take the time to mention this as well. Let the broker know you have sales ability and the confidence to become one of the top producers of the firm. Do not take yourself lightly and no one else will either.

How to Find an Office: Matching Your Needs and Goals

If you know you can motivate yourself, it really is not going to make a big difference where you hang your license. An agent can become a huge success in a small office. However, if you want to achieve the kind of income you want, I believe and many people would agree, you need to be in a large office and preferably one with national recognition. There are several reasons a nationally recognized real estate firm affiliation can be important. Some of these include:

- **National Web site with agent locator**. The advantage of working with a national franchise is national exposure. If you can gain exposure and with large companies such as Keller Williams, Re/Max, and Century 21, there are perks to being within their system as an agent. The agent locator can help you gain clients who wanted to work with a specific firm more than a particular agent.

- **Large referral program enabling agents to gain more agent referrals.** The referral programs used through nationally recognized real estate firms can increase your bottom line but you need to be sure the office handles these referrals fairly. Often one or two agents become recognized within an office as the relocation specialists and then the leads are not divided up at all. You do not want to make a move to a national franchise with expectations of gaining many outside referrals if you do not qualify to receive them; therefore, find out the office's policy on referrals. At the same time, if a broker has an established relocation center within the firm with one or two agents handling the bulk of the business, do not let that one fact alone prevent you from working in that office. A large franchise will have relocation services which they can offer to relocating clients. This is one of the reasons some of the larger corporations will work within a franchise with a strong relocation department. Very often these companies bring business to a firm outside of the relocation program anyway so regardless of how these are handled, you could benefit.

- **Ongoing training opportunities and continuing education.** One reason you sign with a broker is because of continuing education and ongoing support. Find out what they offer.

- **More opportunity to gain corporate accounts and business clients.** Many larger corporations will work only through a nationally recognized franchise, but again find out how these leads are distributed among agents before you base your decision on this one factor.

- **Support of many agents.** Franchises can offer ongoing agent support. From software recommendations to training, the possibilities for learning about real estate from the experts in the field are unlimited, and support is usually just a phone call away or better yet, in-house!

- **More visibility for your listings.** With the national franchises, your listings will gain more exposure because there are so many ways for the company to give an agent visibility, including Web exposure through several Web sites and national advertising.

- **Savvy business campaigns.** From ERA's "If we do not sell your house, we will buy it" to many other lucrative offers, a franchise can offer slogans and campaigns to win over clients for their agents.

- **National advertising.** With franchises, national advertising is never a problem and is one of the reasons so many agents choose a national franchise.

- **National recognition for agents at national franchise conventions and other meetings.** This is why I love the franchises like ERA and Century 21 as well as other large companies. The national conventions are fun and informative and give agents the opportunity to learn from the best in the field. You can find out what works and what does not from people who are doing exactly what you are doing and it is a fun way to network with other real estate agents.

- **Designations to show achievement.** National franchises give achievement awards to their sales associates adding credibility to you and your abilities.

The third year I was in real estate, I had the opportunity to visit Phoenix, Arizona, for a national convention for ERA Real Estate Agents. During the convention, I learned from experts in the field and quickly understood why these agents and sales coaches were able to be so successful. The convention changed my sales techniques and opened my eyes to the career. I do not think I viewed real estate as a lucrative career choice until I rubbed shoulders with some of the best agents in the business. The franchises who sponsor these conventions offer their agents many opportunities to succeed. The conventions are trade shows coupled with dynamic speakers. There is no better place to learn about real estate than through a large meeting of the minds where new agents can see what the true leaders in the industry are doing.

Mom-and-pop real estate offices cannot offer the kind of support and education of larger franchised offices. If you want to be at the top, it only makes sense to work for top companies with national recognition. The advantages far outweigh any disadvantages you may think you see. Still, you can reach top agent status in the smaller offices of your area if you are driven to succeed in your real estate business.

Following are some of the reasons agents prefer to work for small offices. These items are considered to be advantageous for the agents who do prefer to work in close-knit situations.

- Fewer distractions in smaller offices can enable an agent to have more productive time.

- One-on-one attention from the broker can be valuable to an agent starting out in the business.

- Small offices often realize they have less to offer a productive agent so they will give the agent a better split.

- More floor time is not always a big deal if the office does not have many listings. However, in small offices taking floor time often gives the agent the opportunity to become both the listing and selling agent of the properties he or she handles.

- The opportunity for advancement is a big deal for an agent who plans to become a managing broker.

- Small offices provide the opportunity to be the top agent in the office.

New agents view smaller offices as a good place to start with the intent to move to a larger, busier office once he or she knows the business. There are more disadvantages than advantages to do this. It is a hassle anytime you move offices. You are much better off if you choose an office and stay there for as long as you can. If you go to a small office, go there for the right reasons and not just as a starting point. Once you become busy in your business, it is too much trouble to move.

Joining a small office can be advantageous. Some agents join a smaller office in hopes of growing as it grows, and sometimes this happens. I have seen several small offices with two or three agents working steady business. Quickly, the office turned into a large franchised firm with 20 agents. This growth is not the norm but it can happen. It would be very exciting to be part of a growing real estate office and could be fun with the right opportunity!

While you are in search for the perfect office, decide what it is you want. If at some point you know you will not be happy handing over a large percent of your commissions to a broker, look at an office that offers an 80/20 split or higher. There are many 100 percent concept offices out there now. Consider working with one of these offices before you sign on with a broker who offers little for a 60/40 split.

The greatest disadvantage in the 100 percent offices for a new agent is whether you can make it on your own until the sales begin to roll in. Often, this is where a large office with a less desirable agent/broker split can be more advantageous because it is very hard to manage desk fees, advertising and other things you are expected to pay as an agent in a 100 percent office. If you have the funds to support yourself until your first check is secured, then a 100 percent office is one of the best situations you can have as a top producing agent.

Why You Do Not Want to Specialize in This Business As a New Agent

While becoming recognized for a special concentration in real estate is not necessarily a bad thing, it can be for a new agent with no experience whatsoever, especially if you are a newbie going straight into the back-biting world of commercial real estate. I took a hard lesson from a commercial agent in our area once. He was not only shrewd but he left a very bad impression among other agents, especially women. In fact, even though it cost me a very large sale, I refused to deal with him because he was so condescending and played the male chauvinistic card with me. The "honey" and "baby" thing was not too appealing as he tried to woo my clients.

New agents who enter into the world of commercial real estate will find the arms of the others (who think they own the market) crossed firmly to indicate you are not welcome and you are not wanted which is why specializing in commercial real estate as a new agent is not recommended. However, you will have the opportunity to show commercial real estate so you want to learn all you can about it. Even though you will be able to show and sell commercial listings, to be considered a true professional in the area of commercial real estate, you will want to gain your CCMI designation showing you are recognized as an expert in commercial dealings.

Gaining the CCMI designation should be on your list of things to do at some point but going after this particular designation immediately is not necessary. In fact, all new agents need other experiences besides the highly coveted commercial experience.

The chance of bigger and better things is why I strongly urge agents not to limit their sales and listing goals to residential sales. As a new agent, in all likelihood you will find your real estate fortune in residential sales but you never want to be limited to residential by signing on with a real estate firm known solely for residential listings.

If you are affiliated with an office that has a good mix of commercial listings, residential, residential with acreage, and vacant land; doors will open to many opportunities. As a new agent, you really need a chance to see it all and do it all while building your business. If you work in an office with a good mix of listings and a *multitude* of listings, you will gain much needed experience. Also, you will have many opportunities for some dynamite floor calls so make sure you take advantage of every floor time opportunity!

Another thing you do not want to do is to become recognized as a buyer's agent or a listing agent. My family members involved in the business sell and list property so they work with buyers and sellers. Every *successful* real estate agent I know sells and lists property. You do not want to become one or the other but do both so you will be considered the best all-around agent! In some cases, agents do produce better working with one or the other, but why limit yourself?

Do keep in mind, as a listing agent; you are obtaining listings for everyone with access to the MLS to show. If you can become a top listing agent, you will secure the income you want much faster than if you show more property than you list. Choose an office with a good mix of listings, and listing all properties will be a viable option for you.

Make a Decision

Once you decide where you will be comfortable, it is time to sit down with the broker of the office where you want to work and negotiate. Nothing is set in stone until you sign your contract with the office's managing broker. If the managing broker offers you a 70/30 split and you know this to be typical for the office, still push the envelope. Ask for 75/25. Explain you have really given it some thought and you know what you are capable of producing. Tell the broker you feel 75/25 is a fair split considering your commitment to your career and your dedication to success. Handle this professionally and you will likely be able to increase whatever it is the broker has offered you. In the worst case scenario, you should at least be able to work on a graduated scale where you can increase your commission at sales milestones.

When you sit down with a broker, discuss everything from signage to advertising. Know what you are expected to pay for out of pocket and what the real estate firm will take care of for you. You need to have a clear understanding of floor duty schedules, training, continuing education, licensing issues, and MLS dues. Also, most offices have a policy and procedure manual as well as training materials for new agents so take the time to explore them. If you have the option to have a private office versus a shared cubicle, it is highly recommended for you to consider the private office over a shared desk unless it comes with a hefty fee. If you have a designated room in your home for a home-office, do not pay a desk fee to have a private office at the real estate firm. Just make sure you have a place to meet privately with your clients in the office when you need confidential meeting space.

After you have decided which firm you want to join and both

you and the broker are comfortable with the arrangement, it is time to get to work. Send out thank-you notes to all of the brokers you considered working with thanking them for their time. If you can afford to do so, send them a basket of candies or even drop by some cookies with a thank-you note attached. You want to be on good terms with everyone in the business so when the opportunity comes along for the broker or his agents to show your listed properties, they are glad to do it.

You have an office and a good idea of a real estate agent's job description. Now all you need to do is to set up your business and get busy with becoming the top selling and listing agent in your area. With your license hanging on the wall of any real estate firm, there is no time for procrastination. Now it is just about action.

IMPORTANT TIPS from chapter three

1. Be money-driven when you sit down with a broker to discuss your agent-broker split. Remember, managing brokers are money-inspired and there is no reason you cannot be money-minded as well.

2. When interviewing brokers in real estate offices, let them know you are career-oriented. It may make a difference in the split the broker will offer to you.

3. Negotiate all splits. Do not agree to anything until you have tried to increase whatever split is offered on the table. Use the "one hand on the door" sales technique when discussing splits and you may be able to get the split you are looking for in real estate.

4. Know what your broker covers in any advertising fee they attach to agent commissions.

5. What does the broker offer agents in the office in exchange for the agent's being able to hang a license on the wall of the broker office?

6. Know what training is provided in each office you are considering as well as any continuing education. Ask if the broker pays for any of the training or education.

7. Take into consideration all aspects when you compare offices. Look at the split, number of listings they have, how much floor time you will be able to take, and all aspects of the office before you sign on with any real estate firm.

chapter four

Setting Up Your World-Class Real Estate Business

After you choose your office, you should be ready to organize your business. You need to decide first if you are going to conduct the majority of your business from home or from the real estate firm's office. If you choose to set up your main office from home, you need to be well prepared. A home computer and printer are a must; a fax machine which can also double as a copier to produce single copies will come in handy too. You will need supplies ranging from pens and paper clips to your real estate firm's sales contracts/offers to purchase and final walk-through sheets. You should be able to gather a handful of forms for your home office if you choose to work from home. Many of the forms you need in real estate can be found online, making a home office more practical. A good laptop computer is highly recommended but may not be affordable in the early stages of your career.

Regardless of where you decide to conduct your business, you need to keep training material and motivational reading material nearby for easy reference. In the appendix, you will find a list of suggested reading for all new real estate agents, and I suggest

you begin collecting these books as soon as you can and then—
actually read them!

Other Business Matters

There are many areas often overlooked when setting up a real
estate business. Many new agents are often amazed at the fees
involved just to obtain their real estate license, much less just to
get started in the business of selling real estate. Below, you will
find a list of expenses you can expect before hanging your license
on the wall of a real estate broker. Each of the following will vary
from state to state, and the best way to find out what you need
to know in regards to fees is to check with real estate schools in
your area as well as with your broker upon signing on with a real
estate firm.

- Real estate course to prepare agents for pre-license exam

- Real estate exam fees

- Licensing fees

- MLS dues for the agent's local area

- Local board dues (if any, in addition to the MLS dues)

- Vehicle insurance and coverage

- Errors and omissions

One word of caution for individuals starting out into the world
of real estate in regards to real estate schools. Beware of online
courses which promise to help you ace your real estate exam.
Some are only study guide programs, and your state will probably

not honor the course as a satisfactory means of preparing for the exam.

Before you begin life as an active real estate agent, take a moment to find a good accountant. There are many tax advantages in having a home office, and an accountant will be able to share those with you. Also, you want to know what you can and cannot use for deductions at tax time. An accountant will be able to advise you which receipts you will need to keep from your mileage and general business expenses.

Setting Up Your Advertising and Marketing Budget

When you first become a real estate agent, you need to recognize your need for self-promotion. Your office should place an advertisement in your local newspaper announcing your affiliation with their firm, but if they do not pick up the cost for it, you will need to do so. A simple quarter-page ad with your picture and a simple biography will do. However, think more along the lines of press release rather than biography. Now would be a good time to order your business cards, too. Make sure you include only the phone numbers of the phones you plan to answer and make sure you do not list a cell phone number right now if you know you are going to be on a tight budget in the early stages of your career. Give some thought to your availability too. What hours do you want to be available? If you do, then make all of your phone numbers available to your clients.

Kay White

"It is tough when you are trying to market yourself in this business. There is always a good opportunity to gain more exposure, a real challenge for new real estate agents because they cannot possibly afford everything they are presented in the beginning. New agents on a tight budget should talk to other agents about what worked for them before they begin advertising. Talk to someone who knows what works for your area."

Kay White
kwhite5048@earthlink.net
www.tricityareaproperties.com

Advertising can be the death of sales if you cannot afford it. You need to set up an advertising budget based on your income generated from your real estate closings. When you first start out in business, you will not have any real estate closings so you will not have any money for an advertising budget unless you draw from your personal finances. I recommend taking a loan from your personal bank account if you can. If you are in good shape financially when you begin your real estate career, you should be able to afford to loan your business account $3,000, and you really do not need any more than that to start your business. Many agents start with far less than that!

Before you start your business, set up a separate business account to manage your business banking. The account will help you later because you can pay for all of your promotional materials, mail campaigns, marketing, and advertising needs from your business account, and it makes budgeting easier. I know some agents who paid themselves out of their business account. For example, since the business is so volatile, they deposited all of their commissions into their business account and paid themselves a weekly salary. At the end of the year, they would take a large bonus. If you are disciplined to do this, it is a great method to incorporate to ensure you have an income during any unavoidable down-times or dry-spells.

When you are ready to go to work, very soon after signing on with a real estate broker, you will be able to set up an effective advertising budget based on a percentage of your sales. I used a 10 percent rule of thumb at the beginning of my real estate career based on the advice of another agent but later discovered the advertising I did could easily be supported with 5 percent of my commission. For instance, if you sell a $50,000 home and you are the listing and selling agent receiving a 5 percent commission on an 80/20 split, your take would be $2,000. You would take $100 and add it to your advertising budget for the following month based on a 5 percent structure for advertising. If you are a $250,000-a-month agent who sells homes consistently, you would likely contribute $300 to $600 per month to your advertising budget depending on your split and what percentage you use as a guideline for your budget. In most areas, $600 per month would be a little higher than the average but in some areas, you would likely need to adjust this to an even higher percentage particularly if you are responsible for placing your own homes' magazine advertisements and open house ads in a newspaper.

After you set up your budget, call around and check with local newspapers and trade papers to see what their advertising rates are. Check rates on television advertisements and call billboard companies for their rates. Have all important advertising rates at your fingertips should you need to know them for budgeting purposes. Check with all of the homes magazines and brochure printers in your area for rates on these materials as well. After you get the rates, talk to other agents and see what type of advertising they do and ask if they mind sharing with you the percent of their return.

Pay attention to their responses and make notes in your advertising file of what seems to work for some real estate agents and what does not so you will be able to consider the information later. Use the successes and failures of others to help you learn how to manage your own business especially when it comes to advertising.

Another word of advice on advertising is to negotiate your advertising rates. If you are going to be spending many advertising dollars in a particular medium, take the initiative to negotiate your rates down. You should be able to realize some substantial discounts after you begin to advertise.

Planning Your Continuing Education

As an agent, nothing can be more embarrassing than for a required class to come up that you need to have and you do not have the money to take the class. When you are setting up your marketing and advertising budget, you should allot as much money for real estate continuing education and resource materials such as how-to books and sales materials. You also need to find out what your state requirements are for continuing education and what your broker requires in the form of training and continuing education and then plan for educational needs.

Something to keep in mind throughout your real estate career is that you can always take the classes you will need for continuing education a little early in most cases. If you know you are going to need another 15 hours for your continuing education, do not wait until the last minute of the last hour to get it accomplished. Find out what you need to do before the deadline and sign up early for your classes. In many cases, continuing education can be accomplished online. However, it may be necessary to reserve a seat and attend classes.

Depending on your location, your local area may see a decline in real estate sales one particular month out of the year, affording you an opportunity to check into classes in continuing education and gaining certifications, such as Certified Residential Specialist. Remember, costs of classes may be high, and when you are behind in meeting your requirements, they can add up for a new agent. Plan ahead for these costs and for the certifications you want to possess. Check with other agents who hold various designations and become well-informed on all aspects of an agent's education.

Introducing Yourself to the Business Community

After you are settled into your new office, there are some things you must do immediately to begin to establish yourself in the real estate community and the business community in general. If your office carries many extra home magazines, take a large stack of them and attach your business card to the front cover. Then hit the road and begin to place these magazines as well as some of your business cards. Some restaurants have a cashier area where you check out and will allow business cards to be placed on their counter. Ask whether you can do this and then use your creative juices to find other places to put your business cards and home magazines. Following are some ideas.

- Beauty salons are excellent businesses to place homes magazines. You can place them on the coffee tables with all of the hair styling books.

- Business cards can be placed in attorney's offices with permission.

- Home magazines placed with the magazines on tables in a doctor's office work well for leads.

- Place your business cards in break rooms at large manufacturing plants if they are allowed.

- Stop by all the car dealerships in your area and ask if you can place homes magazines in the body shop lounge and waiting areas.

- Again, restaurants are excellent for business cards and some of them may have areas where you could leave your homes magazines, too.

- Drug store counters are excellent for business cards.

- Use the billboards at grocery stores and Wal-Mart to pin up your business cards.

Basically, anywhere you know there is a flow of traffic, you should want to try to place your business cards and homes magazines. This should be a relatively inexpensive way to promote yourself as a real estate professional ready for business.

Margie Larkins

"When agents first get into the real estate business, they need to let other people know what they are doing. It is important to contact everyone you know and tell them you are in real estate and let them know you will be there for them when they need you. You must circulate to percolate."

MARGIE LARKINS   423-246-5700
margielarkins@realtor.com

"We Specialize in Personalized Service"
Serving East Tennessee for over 30 Years

The Coming Out Party

Every agent needs a coming out party! This is a party you do not want to miss having when you first join an office. Talk to your managing broker and see if it will be a problem to serve refreshments and invite contractors to stop by. If it is a problem because of conflicts of interest with other agents or for whatever reason, move the party to a local restaurant. You can pull this off without a large expense if you choose a family-style or buffet-style restaurant with a private room. Invite someone in the building industry to speak to your contractors who show up and, of course, pick up their tab for lunch. Truthfully, everyone loves a free lunch so if you want to have a huge turn-out for your coming out party, then opt for a luncheon rather than having an open house at your office unless your budget is extremely tight.

If done properly, the coming out party will give your business a fantastic lift-off, and you will be surprised at how quickly you will be gaining business! Take a look at the following suggestions for a successful coming out party:

- The first thing is to decide where you want to have your luncheon. If at all possible, choose a restaurant close to several large up and coming home developments so it is handy for the market you are trying to reach—the contractors building in these subdivisions!

- Next, contact a local building supplier or flooring company and explain to them what you are doing and invite them to speak to your group of contractors. Remind the person you talk with to bring their own business cards and promotional tools. After all, this is a great opportunity for them, too.

- Decide on a date and send out invitations to every contractor or developer in your area.

- Remember to invite your broker.

- Before the big day arrives, design and print brochures that introduce you briefly and list area subdivisions with vacant lots and prices as well as large tracts of land perfect for subdividing. The listings do not need to be your listings. This is just a sheet to show the builders what vacant lots are available for them to consider at a later date. Who knows, they may already be in the market for their next building site!

- On the big day, wear a professional-looking suit (and name tag if possible) and wait for your guests to arrive. Make sure you greet every guest personally with a friendly smile and a handshake.

- When everyone is there, introduce yourself as the newest member of the XYZ Real Estate Firm and give a brief history about yourself. Toastmasters would be a great group to attend prior to your big coming out party if you have trouble speaking in front of groups. Most Toastmasters meet regularly and even one meeting can provide you with tips to help you overcome the jitters if you need the encouragement.

- After you have talked for a few minutes, introduce your guest speaker and sit down and relax. The speaker should be prepared to talk about something of interest to your guests.

- Ideally, your speaker will limit his presentation to 20 minutes. Keep in mind, in the middle of the day, a contractor will probably be unable to give you no more than an hour so keep your entire luncheon moving along.

- After the speaker is finished, you should take the floor again and thank the contractors for coming, ask them to take along the brochure they found at their place setting, and ask for their future business. If you do not ask for their business, why would a contractor think you could sell one of their homes? Ask for what you want and tell them how hard you are willing to work for your clients. Be sure to mention the list of vacant land and recommend they call you if they see a listing that looks appealing. Remind your group you are able to show anything listed in the multiple listings. Often people do not even know this unless you tell them.

You may think this is carrying the pursuit of gaining business too far but if you want to build a world-class real estate business, you need to be direct. When the contractors receive your invitation for lunch, they will know you want their business. If they are locked in with another real estate agent in the business and have loyalties to uphold, they will likely decline the invitation. However, nothing ventured, nothing gained and as a new agent you need contacts. This is a great way to get them.

If possible, ask for the contractors who attend the luncheon to provide you with a list of spec homes they have for sale or ask them for the name of the subdivisions where they prefer to build. Use this information later to take new clients to these builders for one time showings. What a way to make an impression if you have a buyer looking for a house and you call a contractor with a client ready to buy one of his houses! You will have this builder's attention.

After the luncheon, send out thank you notes to the contractors who showed up and thank them for coming to your luncheon and enclose your business card. Remind them if they ever need a full-time real estate agent, you would like to have the opportunity to *earn* their business.

If you had a contractors who declined the invitation, pay attention to whether they already work with an agent and if they do not, call them up and invite them to lunch in the future, after your first sale!

IMPORTANT TIPS from chapter four

1. Know what expenses you will have as an agent. What will your dues be and how much will it cost to run your business most effectively?

2. Talk to an accountant before you start your new career.

3. Use 10 percent of your income for marketing and advertising when you first start out and adjust this percentage after you determine how much you will need for your budget.

4. Negotiate with advertisers for the best rates.

5. Plan ahead for your continuing education.

6. Introduce yourself to the community. How can you expect everyone to know where to find you if you do not let them know where you are and what you are doing?

7. Have a coming-out party and get to know the contractors in your community.

8. Remind everyone you meet that you can show any property listed in the Multiple Listings.

chapter five

Step-by-Step Business Plan for Success

E veryone wants to be successful in a new career but with a handful of agents in any given area doing the vast majority of the business, this is not always the case. If you are going to be successful in real estate, you need to make plans to be successful and then work your plan until you are and then work it again. Follow this plan and you will become successful in real estate but the trick here is to stay at the top once you reach the peak. You will find you never have to worry about a steady flow of business if you just remain consistent with a plan we will start to put into motion right now.

The Pre-Planning Stages

Before we go any further, I want you to decide right now what you want from your real estate career. What is it that drove you into the throes of one of the most volatile businesses in the world? What appeals to you about being paid only if you make a sale? Why do you want to be a real estate agent? What are your short-term and long-term career goals?

Stop here and grab a new journal to use as a business journal to document your first year of real estate. Answer these questions on paper and refer to them often:

- **Why did I obtain a real estate license?** There has to be a reason. What was it? Did you want flexibility in scheduling? Do you think agents get rich? Why did you choose real estate for a career path? Throughout your real estate career, you need to know your reason because it will guide you into a successful first year in the business and can give purpose your entire career.

- **How much money do I want to make in my first year of real estate?** Be realistic. Then, be unrealistic and try to reach a happy medium. Everyone knows their own limitations. Take a good, hard look at your expectations for your career and look at what you want to earn as well as what you need to earn. Then decide on what you will earn. Whatever figure comes to mind, I want you to be able to achieve that amount so set a goal you can achieve.

- **Why is it important to me to become the top agent** in my first year of real estate — what do I want to gain from it?

- **Many agents want to become a top agent for reasons other than money.** Why do *you* want to be a top agent? Is it for the competition or to manage your ego? Is it because of the money? There is nothing wrong with your reason as long as you know what it is! For me, I wanted the money. I also liked having the most listings in the offices where I worked but even that was because of the money I wanted.

- **How much real estate do I want to sell?** Let me give you a dose of reality. As mentioned earlier, often a million dollar producer just earns an average income of around $40,000. How much you want to earn will determine how much real estate you want to sell. If you sell three million dollars in real estate, based on varying commission structures, your split and other factors, you will earn anywhere from $100,000 to around $140,000. So, how much do you want to sell? How are you going to earn the income you want?

- **What are you willing to do to become successful?** Ask yourself what you are willing to do, what you are willing to sacrifice and how you will achieve success. You cannot be successful if you do not know why you want to be successful or what is required for you to become successful in real estate. Do you know what it takes? Will you do what it takes?

- **How many hours are you going to be willing to work to achieve your goals?** You must know how many hours you are willing to work per week. You can change this later after a couple of years in the business or maybe 18 months after you start. However, for now, set some business hours and stick to them and be prepared to work hard because it will take many long hours and hard work as a new agent.

- **How many days a week** are you going to work to achieve your goals?

Plan a regular day off each week and stick to it. If you have a family and know you need a couple of days off each week, set up the days now and only change them in extreme circumstances. You need to work long hours during your first year of real estate, but if you work seven days a week from the start, you will burn out. Many people who have gone before you did, and you will be no different regardless of how great the money is.

- **What do you want to do with the money you earn other than simple living expenses and payments for bills?** What dreams do you have? You have to dream. If your dream is only to live and pay bills, you do not have any motivation to become successful. How exciting is it to dream of just paying your bills? What do you want to do with your life? Where do you want to go? What homes do you hope to have? Do you want a nice car? Dare to dream. Then do it in a big way and achieve it.

- **Finish this statement**. My overall career goals are:

If you do not know what you want to do in your career as a real estate agent, you will likely do nothing. If you do not know what you want to earn as a real estate agent, you will likely earn nothing. You must know what your goals are and then you need to know how to meet and exceed those goals.

Part of becoming a success in real estate is going to depend on your making the effort and taking the time to do things no one else will do and being glad to do them. My mother does some of the craziest things for her clients, but she does them because she wants to do them. She is a wonderful cook and she loves to bake delicious cakes. She will take cakes and treats to the clients she has worked with over the past year when the holidays roll around. Naturally, they are surprised to find her on their doorstep a couple of days before Christmas. She gives her customers friendly real estate service with a twist. They never leave her circle of influence, and she never leaves them. She remembers they are her valued clients and treats them as such. Many would say she carries it too far but others would say she is just ensuring she always has a stream of income from the referrals her past clients send her.

When I was in real estate, I had more open houses than almost anyone. I had them every Sunday and many times throughout the entire weekend. It was something that helped me gain the trust and confidence of new home builders, and it enabled me to tap into a market many new agents do not tap into. However, if a client ever received a baked item from me, it was likely bought! I guess every agent must find what makes them stand out and then play on that attribute.

Margie Larkins is an agent in the Tri-Cities Area of Tennessee who has been in business for more than 30 years. Her secrets of success are wide-ranging because Margie knows it takes persistent, patience, and education to stand out in a crowd. Below, you will find advice from her, a true professional in the business.

Margie Larkins

Margie Larkins knows the secrets to success in the real estate business because she has realized tremendous success in the years she has dedicated to the business. When I asked her what it takes to be successful in the real estate business, she immediately knew how to respond. She said, "You have to be dedicated; you have to follow-up with your clients and show them you appreciate them by being available to work when the client is ready for you to help them."

Margie Larkins
margielarkins@realtor.com

"We Specialize in Personalized Service"
Serving East Tennessee for over 30 Years

Developing Your Plan of Action

Before you decide how you are going to work your business, you need to decide how much time you are going to spend each week working your business. We will discuss this more later but you need to find a healthy balance between home and career; otherwise, you will work yourself right out of business and maybe right out of your home life as you know it.

Take this into consideration and then plan when and how much you will work.

- **An agent who controls his or her business** from the very beginning can work appointments around his/her schedule and find a happy medium with life and work. An agent who allows the business to control his/her life ends up without one.

- **Set up normal business hours** based on what you know your schedule tends to be and based on your life's activities. If you do not have children living at home, you should be able to do this without facing too many schedule interruptions. However, if you have school schedules and the activities of others to work around, the flexible scheduling should be worked to your advantage.

- **A suggestion for working agents** is to take one day off during the week when you absolutely refuse to work. You should never work longer than 10 hours a day because the business will consume you and all of your life's activities. However, clients need to know when they can reach you, and if you establish business hours you will find more clients appreciate knowing when they can reach you than there are clients who will see your schedule in an unfavorable light.

- **Typical office hours** could be Sunday through Thursday from 11 a.m. until 9 p.m. or whatever works for you. Remember successful agents work almost every weekend so you need to realize this when you start planning your office hours. Regardless of what you hear from any other agent, if you want to run your business like a business, you need regular working hours. I have talked to many agents about this in the past. I have found the agents without set hours or parameters regarding when they work tend to be unhappy in their career. No one wants to work all of the time no matter what they do for a living!

- **Buy a date book and a large wall calendar for your office**. As you plan your first full year in business, pull out a calendar and go ahead and schedule when you plan to take weekends off or a scheduled vacation. One of the keys to success in your first year of real estate is to plan your calendar year and then work when you plan! If you know there are classes you need or want to take throughout the year, go ahead and pencil in those dates along with any national conventions you want to attend.

- **Find another new agent who will not mind covering for you if you return the favor on occasion**. While you do not want to work as a team with another new agent, you should find a go-getter to swap floor time with you or to cover a last-minute showing for you. If you have more clients than you have time, refer some of them out for a 20 percent referral fee. However, if you do this, recognize the pitfalls we mention in this book.

- Finally, get organized. You will be far more successful if you keep everything neat and organized!

Step-by-Step

You have your calendar in front of you and your date book is open. Now it is time to work out your daily schedules and what you want to plan to do each day in addition to any regular appointments you may have throughout the day. There are many things you will need to do to get your name out in the local area as a licensed real estate agent and to build your business. The important thing to remember is to stay focused on becoming a successful real estate agent and to follow a schedule. Remain consistent and it will pay off for you!

Following is a list of things you must do each and every week along with recommendations on how much time you need to spend doing these things each week. If you work your business with these suggestions, you will see a return on your invested time quickly. Since agents must work their property showings around their client's schedules, plan to execute the following at some point during your day or week without losing focus on your clients. If you will do all of the following, though, you are only ensuring you have an endless flow of business.

- **Usually, a managing broker will send out a floor-duty schedule for the coming month**. Once you receive it, mark on your calendar the days you are scheduled and avoid scheduling property showings during your floor duty. Also, as a new agent, it is a good idea to send out a memo to all of the other agents and announce you are looking for more floor duty shifts. Ask other agents to let you know within three days which shifts you can pick up for them. If you have your primary office at the firm, you can hang out in your office and perform your daily duties. Let the floor agent know if she or he steps out, you will cover their calls. Remember, take all of the floor duty you can because floor duty gives agents an opportunity for sales and listings.

- **Every morning, obtain a local newspaper and at some point during the day, call all of the "for sale by owners" ads listed in the paper**. You should use one of our phone scripts in the appendix for ease in securing an appointment. Never call anyone who has listed in their advertisement "no agents please" because there is usually a good reason for this and you will have plenty other FSBO opportunities through the vacant land and homes listings. However, you can use their phone number to locate their mailing address. Send the homeowner your business card and a market comparison of their home. See the appendix for a sample letter to enclose as well. If you have a mailing list, and you should, add the homeowner to your mailing list. Send out newsletters to everyone on your mailing list. If you are part of a national franchise, you can often obtain newsletters through the corporate offices; if not, you can create your own.

- **Canvass for business**. There is an agent tool no one should be without. It is the Blue Book which breaks down the local area by community. This is handy for you because it lists the homeowner, the street address, and phone number. You can use this to help you with canvassing. Go ahead and order one of these books and plan to canvass a couple of hours, two days a week. Doing so will set you apart from other agents in your area.

- **When you have some listings, you will be able to hold open houses.** I have had very little luck with Saturday open houses unless the home was in a high traffic area, but Sunday open houses are usually busy. Until you have some listings of your own, approach another agent and ask them if they need help with any of their open houses. Make sure you stipulate you will be glad to take one on your own. You do not want to hang out at an open house with another agent and then watch as they make the commission on the sale (and yes, this happens). Once you have your own listings, you can drop a few flyers about the home to some of the local businesses you know that employ many individuals or send out the flyers to homeowners in an area where you have noticed many for sale signs. Promote your open houses in the newspaper and through other creative means.

- **Each morning, it is imperative that you check the MLS (multiple listing service) for new listings that any one of your buyers might find appealing**. Send the listing sheet to them by e-mail if you see something you know they will like. There are some automated options offered through some MLS boards so you need to check for them also. If you can have buyers receive the listing automatically, you can save a few steps, but you should always call your client and see what they thought of the new listing, which they received an e-mail notice, and see if they want to see the property.

- **Spend about two hours a week on promotional planning and advertisement.** Planning upcoming promotions, such as drawings for real estate agents and clients, and other promotions along with advertising can be helpful.

Plan to take a new home builder out to lunch or contact an apartment complex manager and ask if you can meet with them to discuss placing your business cards in the complex. Do what it takes to meet the people who can send you business!

- **The day after you get a new listing, you should immediately fax a listing sheet to other area offices**. You can also mail out the listing sheet to top area agents. One thing I highly recommend to new agents is to encourage sellers to place a bonus on the home for the selling agent. If they squirm at the thought of a bonus, explain you will forfeit the opportunity of course, but to entice agents to show the home or piece of property, a bonus added is tempting. I used this often when I was in real estate. When you send out the listing sheet, be sure to highlight the bonus with an appropriate header, "OUTSTANDING $1,000 CASH BONUS TO THE SELLING AGENT."

- **A Web presence is a necessity**. Find someone to build your Web site for you and ask them to teach you how to maintain it. Good agents work constantly at maintaining their Web site, and are savvy about keeping their placement in the top three on the major search engines. We will look at how you can do this later but at least once a day, you should take a look at your Web site. See what you need to do to improve it, check your e-mail, and handle contacts in your virtual world.

- **Always plan at least one promotion per month and work on it as mentioned in the previous chapter.** Luncheons for builders, open houses at a home near a large apartment complex with invitations sent out to the tenants of the complex, and free home buying seminars are great ways to promote yourself as a real estate professional. Use your imagination!

- **In addition to the canvassing and calling FSBOs as mentioned above,** top agents cold call, and we will discuss this later. Since you are starting out in business, cold calls made daily can be a great way to boost your business. See the appendix for phone scripts.

- **Twice a week, you need to go out into the community and replenish your business cards and homes magazine**s. Stop by some new businesses you have had no contact with and find at least a couple of new places to place your cards each week.

- **After you begin to list property, you should designate a time once a week to call the property owner to let them know how it is going, recommend anything** you can to them, and offer any feedback you have received. You will also want to schedule an open house for them if you feel it is important and basically let the seller know what you are doing to sell their house or property.

- **Good agents know it is imperative to touch base with loan officers and title companies** throughout the week for information on any pending sales in the works.

- **If you can afford to use billboards, they are a great tool**. However, if you are going to use billboards, see if you can rotate them every six months for a fresh look.

- **Do not forget to watch wedding announcements in your local newspapers** and if you can obtain a phone number, give the happy couple a call and show them how buying is better than renting.

Use the above suggestions to schedule your real estate calendar and day to day activities.

Remember, as an independent contractor, you have the flexibility to change your schedule somewhat. Just remember to get everything in each and every week to ensure you are consistently building your business.

One of the best ways to build your business will be canvassing. Even if you do not have one of the Blue Books to begin, you can use the Internet or just pinpoint an area to begin canvassing. Some agents call it "canvassing for listings" but often when you canvass enough and you do it correctly, you will find sellers and buyers who want to work with you. The way this works is simple but to be successful you must decide to canvass an area consistently for a year or more.

You can canvass in various ways, but the best way is to choose a condominium complex and start small. First, you send out a letter like our canvassing letter in the appendix and then follow up with a phone call and a series of letters, preferably a newsletter or two and later another phone call. The idea is to get to know the area and introduce the area to you. If you can do this the right way, you will be the first real estate agent anyone in the area will think about when it comes time to list their own home or buy something else.

An agent who can do this successfully will enter a neighborhood into the canvassing cycle and keep the neighborhood in it for a year. Each month, the agent will add another neighborhood or condominium complex into the cycle and start the canvass cycle for group two, and group two will stay in the canvassing cycle for a year. Ideally, at the end of the year, you will have 12 groups cycling, and each time you have one group ready to expire you will evaluate whether the group has pulled enough business for you to continue with the canvassing in that particular area.

Basic Canvassing Cycle

A good basic canvassing cycle works as follows:

Month 1:	Enter a group of 50-100 residential homes into the canvassing cycle and send out a letter of introduction.
Month 2:	Send out your first newsletter.
Month 3:	Call residents in the group to see whether they are thinking of selling or buying. Take anyone out of your canvassing cycle who asks you to put them into a "do not call" status.
Month 4:	Send out your second newsletter.
Month 5:	Send out your third newsletter.
Month 6:	Send out a free market newsletter specific to the general area where you are canvassing. Be sure to include how many homes have recently sold in the area and current home listings in the area. Mention if you have buyers looking for a home in the area.
Month 7:	Send out your fourth newsletter.
Month 8:	Send out your fifth newsletter.

Month 9:	Send out a personalized letter telling the resident about your desire to be their real estate agent and include any investment properties for sale. Show a resident how to invest and make suggestions for great investment opportunities.
Month 10:	Send out your sixth newsletter.
Month 11:	Send out a letter not stating a "good-bye" but asking for the individual to keep you in mind whenever they have a real estate need.
Month 12:	Send out your seventh newsletter which includes a comment card with an option for the homeowners to check if they are interested in staying on your mailing list.

After the 12th month, the group will drop out of your system except for the individuals who have requested to stay on your mailing list. If you have people who have made the initiative to stay on your list, simply re-enter them into your canvassing program with another group or add them to a separate mailing for newsletters only.

Canvassing really can set you apart from other agents in your area, but you must stay on top of it. Starting a canvassing program is pointless if you are not going to dedicate the time needed for it to be a success.

The success of a good canvassing program will depend on your ability to construct friendly letters of introduction, informative newsletters, and a winning script for calling the people on your mailing list.

Something to keep in mind when you call people in your canvassing program is that you want them to like you instantly.

In order for them to do this over the phone, you will need to be friendly and pay attention to their needs and wants. Ask them for suggestions on what they would like to see in their newsletters. Get them involved in your success. Indirectly, home owners can help you build your business if they remember you and you will not be a memorable agent if you do not spend some time getting to know the people in the areas and communities you canvass.

Another way to make canvassing work to the fullest extent is for you to offer incentives for people to send you business. Send out mall gift certificates and dining gift certificates to people who send you business along with a personal thank you note. You will enjoy getting the business you are sent and the people who think of you and send you business will love a token of your appreciation.

IMPORTANT TIPS from chapter five

1. Know why you chose real estate as a career path.

2. Know what it will take to become a million dollar agent.

3. Decide how much you are going to work each day and set business hours.

4. Call FSBOs.

5. Get out in the community and place cards and homes magazines.

6. Obtain a Web site and work at gaining high placement on the Web so you are easily located.

7. Offer to cover another agent when he/she is unavailable and see if he/she will do the same for you. Find someone you can depend on when you are unavailable.

8. Canvass for business and do it consistently.

chapter six

Marketing Your Real Estate Business

One of the first things you need to decide is how you want to market yourself as a real estate agent. Give self-marketing some thought because you want to place your business in a positive light while finding a way to be remembered by others in the industry and within your community.

You need to have a mission statement—something people will remember you by and add it to your Web site and your business cards. It will reflect your marketing approach. Following are some non-traditional ways to market your real estate business that range from pricey to inexpensive forms to get your name out there! These suggestions are wide ranging so you can have some ideas of how to market yourself effectively in different settings.

- **If you want to sell lake property** but you do not live on the lake, you have to find a way to mingle with these homeowners. If you do not own a boat, rent one and the first chance you have, take some drink cozies out to the lake and toss some out to people. You can pull up to their boat, introduce yourself, and toss them some cozies which have your name, mission statement, and phone number along with a company logo. Then, every time the person slides another drink into one of the cozies, they will think of you!

- **Contractors love contractor pencils**. You can have a hardware store pre-order these for you and you will be able to hand them out to contractors you visit on the job sites. Make sure you have your name and phone number on them so they know where they can find this information when they are ready to list their spec house.

- **Sponsor a baseball little league team**. Go out and watch some of their games. There is no better way to become better known in a small community than to support youth activities in the area. You will just need to supply shirts and caps and then you can take a cooler full of drinks out to the game a couple of times or treat them to pizza after a big game! This is a profitable tool to use if there are several schools and little leagues in your area. Choose several teams to sponsor throughout the year and stay close to those you support. When you are supporting a community's youth, they will remember you when it is time to buy or sell their home.

- **Billboards are expensive** but if you choose to use them, do it consistently. Sign a six-month lease on one and include a catchy mission statement or slogan.

- **Hold seminars**. Conduct well-planned seminars for new homeowners and first-time home buyers on how to buy homes with no money down. Do not charge for them, of course, because your goal is to gain business. You should put some thought into when and where you will have them. Advertise your seminar and ask a mortgage professional to help you. Have them available to answer questions and provide information on loans and mortgages. Typically, you want to provide a two-or three-hour seminar one night during the week or on a Saturday morning for the best turnout possible. Offer freebies from area businesses.

- **Any time you are invited to speak about your business, do it!** I was invited to speak at a local credit union once and it proved beneficial. I ended up working with three buyers out of about ten couples so I thought it was definitely worth my time. Know what the theme of the meeting or luncheon is and put thought into your speech. Practice at home and use cheat notes. Also, do not forget to take material to hand out to attendees. You want to ensure that future clients remember your name and know how to reach you.

As a real estate professional, it is important for you to be viewed as a professional by your community. Get out there and get busy. Let people know you are a full-time agent who is educated on all areas of the business and do what it takes to become as educated as you can on all aspects of the business. I cannot stress enough how important holding seminars in your area can be. Below, you will find topics and suggestions for them and it is recommended from the beginning of your career that you hold these classes or seminars at least twice a year. Becoming known as the professional whom buyers and sellers can rely on is very important and will give you a competitive edge. Use these suggestions as topics and build up your own topics and ideas.

1. **How to buy** property with no money down

2. **How to invest** in real estate

3. **What helps** and what will not when preparing your home to sell or "staging your home"

4. **How to sell** your home within 120 days

5. **Buying** your first home

6. **Downsizing** and finding the home perfect for retirement

7. **Buying** real estate in resort areas

8. **Collecting** real estate for financial gain

As you can see, there are many areas you can cover in a seminar. Remember, plan ahead with printed materials, business cards, and listing sheets of available listings. For example, if your seminar is on how to buy property with no money down, provide information on homes listed as available for no-money-down purchases or lease purchases. Always have your next class planned so you can announce it and ask your audience to bring a friend. Serve light refreshments and offer a 10- or 15-minute break during the seminar to allow your audience to mingle. Provide name tags and always allow the seminar or class to be interactive so your guests can ask questions and find answers.

Deciding How You Want to Market Yourself

As an agent, you will have many opportunities to market yourself and your business. Every advertising agent in the world will stop by to say hello to you when you first begin in the business and if they do not visit on the beginning, they will as soon as you begin to show signs of a busy and successful real estate agent. While I can offer you many ideas for successful marketing campaigns, ultimately you will need to come up with something which works best for you.

When I was out in the field working, I used to pass out ball caps at the local livestock markets. Since I grew up on a cattle farm, I knew the business I really wanted tended to be acres and acres of scenic farm land. Since I also worked with contractors, the ball caps worked because in the hot sun, these things were easy to put on whenever I stopped by a job site. For me, the caps were fun to hand out and they kept my name out in front of the public. For you, something else like the contractor pencils or drink cozies might work best.

There are some things that do not work well. Unless you are sponsoring a sports team, avoid T-shirts. They shrink, they fade, and they wear out. Finally, T-shirts are very expensive to produce when other things can be done with a better rate of success. Use your thinking cap and decide what it is that will work for you and the market you are trying to reach.

Finding a Way To Be Remembered and Recognized

The agent who was Rookie of the Year for the Corporate ERA firm the year I went to Phoenix for the conference was the master of self-promotion. However, he took it to the extreme. He became known as the agent available 24 hours a day, seven days a week and became the overworked Rookie of the Year with about $10 million in sales. I remember a lot about him and what he did to make his first year a success and the thing that stood out most about him was his ideas for self-promotion. He was tireless and it paid off.

The best thing you can do for yourself as a new agent is to find a way to stand out, search for a way to be remembered, and become recognizable in a crowded room as the go-to real estate agent. If this means being on a few billboards around town with a catchy slogan and a million dollar agent smile, do it. If it means sponsoring a little league team in baseball, basketball, and football, do it. Whatever it takes, make it your mission to become a recognized force in the real estate community. Be an agent people remember.

In Front of Everyone All of the Time

Top real estate agents have discovered the best way to market their businesses is simply being visible—not always in the physical sense. As an agent, it is important to have your name out in the community all of the time in many different facets and if you can promote yourself through canvassing efforts, you will enjoy rampant success with name recognition. When using the canvassing system, make sure you place your business card with photo in everything you send out by mail and when using newsletters, include your photo and contact information. Use every opportunity to send out your contact information and include it in everything you do.

This is why it is so important to attend a couple of ball games if you sponsor a team or coach a little league team. People want *to know you* and not just your name. If you are out in the community, they will know you. If your name is everywhere, they will remember you and if your photograph is out there, they will recognize you. You want to be in front of as many people as often as you can— even if in name only.

Marketing Your Business and Yourself

While marketing your business and yourself to your area, remember to focus on the areas that are most appealing to you as an agent. If you are uncomfortable around cattle and horses, it is would be ridiculous for you to wade through cattle barns when you show properties to potential ranchers. At the same time, if you find you simply need more experience showing commercial property because you do not understand everything you should pertaining to commercial real estate, wait until you do before you try to market yourself as a commercial real estate agent. Better yet, wait until you obtain your CCMI before focusing marketing efforts in a commercial direction. Even though you do not want to limit yourself to a niche market, you do not want your marketing efforts to be directed toward an area you have no interest in.

Without a marketing background, you will make some marketing and advertising mistakes. Even with a background in marketing, you will make some mistakes but planning ahead and working to get the most out of your marketing and advertising efforts will pay off handsomely for you in the future.

Remember, as a new agent, you do not want to spend money on your marketing and advertising campaigns. Keep costs down by using creative measures to generate the most sales and listings for your efforts. Word of mouth is the most effective form of advertising, and if you are low on cash, the best way to obtain business is to get out and ask for it even if it means going door to door and canvassing on foot. With a winning personality and charisma, you will find the business. Once you get it, just be bound and determined to make a client for life!

IMPORTANT TIPS from chapter six

1. Decide how you want to market yourself and your business.

2 Find the marketing tools that will work best for you.

3. Hold seminars and establish yourself as an authority in the real estate business.

4. Throw your marketing into areas where you want to work.

5. Be an agent people can remember.

6. Find a way to stand out in your community.

7. Network, Network, Network.

8. Never turn down an opportunity to speak on your profession.

chapter seven

Becoming the Go-To Agent

I do not envy new real estate agents. In a feast or famine career, the first year for new agents is not only tough and unpredictable but it can be downright discouraging. However, if you stay focused on your goals and dreams of being a million dollar agent, everything else will fall in line. You have probably heard several old adages related to careers and becoming successful. When I was in real estate I used to hear the same one over and over again from the same agent. She would remind me to "keep doing what you're doing, and the sales will come". She would walk by my office and peek in on me to let me know this and eventually, they did come and the listings followed. In fact, I outsold this agent every year while I was in real estate and yet, I still loved to hear her advice and called her for it long after I left the office where she hung her license. She also told me, "Love what you are doing, and the money will follow." I believe you must have a love for real estate as much as the love of the business itself to be successful.

For you to become a successful real estate agent, you need to make up your mind you are already a huge success. The first year of your real estate career is typically the worst but it can vary greatly because of market conditions and other factors which cause sales to fluctuate. Remember, if you enter into your new career believing your first year in the business will be the worst year, guess what? It will be. On the flip side, if you positively affirm it will be your best year you will not let yourself down!

Establishing Yourself As the Go-To Agent

In this business more than any other, if you are going to be successful, you need to appear successful. This adage is truer in the real estate community than any other for several reasons. First of all, misery does love company and in an industry where a small percent of agents take home the largest portion of agent commissions, there is misery out there if you want to find it, but you will be better off avoiding the office inner circle made up of the good-time agents who go broke in this business. Learn to rub shoulders with successful people. If you want to be successful, you will learn more from successful agents who are willing to work for their business than the inner circle working for the next cocktail party.

When I was in real estate, I worked for one of the largest offices in Kingsport during my first and second years in the business. Our broker started out trying very hard to encourage agents. She arranged fun property tours, informative and uplifting sales meetings, and was the best broker I ever had—only I did not realize it at the time. Office politics did her in. Two agents in the office were like a cancer to me. I preferred to work in the office, but because these agents fostered conflict at all times I could not get anything done there. A couple of us left because of them, and it was the beginning of the end for the broker. Quickly, all agents abandoned her because these two agents interfered with everyone's business.

My point is it is not worth it for you to become too chummy with the other agents in your office. If you never become too involved in office politics, if there is a blow-up in the office, you will likely be unaware of it. Even if you are aware of it, chances are it will not have an effect on your business. If it does, you can move and suffer no loss.

Whether you choose to join a small or a large office, try to keep everything professional. In my opinion, you should not work in teams because then you set yourself up to be judged on the reputation of another person. Agents who do not want to work their own business are always on the look out to team up with a more productive agent. Before you consider any team concept, ask yourself how this 'team concept' will benefit you. The only team concept I have ever known to work has been a large team of multiple agents and not the powerful teaming of two.

Be likeable and professional. People like to do business with people they like who are successful. Would you rather buy a home from an established agent who knew the business of real estate rather than work with a new agent who may not know all of the ins and outs of taking your purchase to the closing table effectively? Sure you would! However, if you avoid office cliques and befriend successful people, you will become recognized as a successful person. In fact, the little detail of your being a new agent will not occur to the person who chooses to do business with you. After all, you must have something to offer and know everything your client needs to know about real estate if you are associated with million dollar producers. Also, if you are working your business professionally, and marketing yourself successfully, you will find all of the business you can handle because people really will not notice how long you have been in the real estate business.

There are some things you can do to stand out in a crowd of real estate agents and you need to decide to start doing them from the very beginning of your career. Consider the following:

- **Appear to be easygoing** even if you are not. Never let anyone outside your immediate family see you when you are discouraged, mad, or coming unglued. NEVER. A wise real estate investor told me a long time ago, "Your problem is you are a hot-head and if you do not keep it in check, it will get the best of you." From that day forward, I kept my temper in check because this investor was right. I was a hot-head and if he noticed it, others would soon notice it too. I just lucked out that he was one of my first clients who thought enough of me to tell me. If you are going to blow a fuse, never do it in public and remember, if you do, agents will whisper to everyone about your little fit. You need a bullet-proof vest in this back-biting business and if you step out of line, it will follow you because your competition will ensure that it does.

- **You have to remember**, you are your business. If you have a good reputation in business, it becomes your personal reputation and vise versa. In fact, the two become so entwined it is impossible in many cases to separate them.

- **Be excited**, optimistic, and enthusiastic about your business, but do not be a phony.

- **Real estate enables you to work for yourself**. This means you do not have to go to work if you do not want to go and it is not mandatory to return your phone calls. You do not have to show up for a listing presentation or even keep your appointments. After all, you are self-employed. You can do what you want to do. Take this approach and failure will find you. Smart agents know that to become a million dollar agent takes self-discipline. You must be able to be a mature business owner. Remember it only takes a little more effort to be a successful million dollar real estate than it takes to be a mediocre agent. The mediocre agent will spend about as much time as you do in the office. The difference will be in how you handle your business, how you follow a consistent routine designed to make you successful, and how others will soon recognize you from all of your active campaigns and efforts. The true difference will be that when you are working, you will actually work whereas the mediocre agent will sit waiting for work to land in his lap.

- **Community involvement** can be very important in becoming a recognized agent. We talked about how you should sponsor a little league recreational sports team, but there are many other things you can and should do to help in your community. You should join the Chamber of Commerce and any other community organizations. Men may become active in the Lions Club or Ruritan Club and find clients there. Likewise, women who join Junior League or another women's organization or club will find future business from the ladies they meet in these clubs. Networking is best when you are having fun doing something for a good cause so volunteer within your community and get busy finding ways to meet new people.

- **Heed the words,** "Think outside the box." If you are going to stand out in this business, be a creative thinker, an active doer, and a go-getter! Take the initiative to try everything once in your business. See what advertising works, try new marketing campaigns, and work on new promotions. What works for you in the area where you work? Find out what other successful people are doing in their real estate business in other areas and adapt it to your area and marketplace. Try almost anything once.

Establishing yourself as the go-to agent in your area is not an easy task but you can make it look easy. One thing to keep in mind is that people like to deal with genuine people who are interested in them as people. You can become a people-pleaser, even a yes-man but unless you are genuinely interested in people, you will never be able to realize your full potential. Keep this advice in mind as you are becoming the go-to agent:

- **Clients do not want to be sold a house.** They want to buy a house.

- **Clients do not want to be viewed as your lifeline or your next paycheck**. They do not want to feel like they are the only thing standing in between you and the end of your career. Do not make a client feel like you need to sell them a property.

- **Real estate investments and purchases are the largest purchases anyone is likely to make**. Do not be too pushy as a salesperson. Have a little faith in the loyalty your clients have to you. When they are ready to buy, they will buy from you because you have earned their trust and earned their business. If you become too pushy, especially when you are dealing with a huge investment, you will lose your clients and when you lose a client, they often spread word of mouth 'warnings' rather than something more positive.

- **Show an interest in what your clients are saying to you.** If you show an interest in what they are saying, you will discover their hot buttons. You will discover why they want a home in a certain area, why they prefer a patio over a deck, and many other things. If you pay attention to what you are being told, you can later use these things to help you close on a deal when the client is weighing the pros and cons of several properties.

- **Become likeable and like your clients**. Some of us will have more trouble with this than others, but do it anyway. Like your clients and become a person to be liked. Even if you do not like them, find a good quality about them to make them tolerable throughout your real estate transaction.

- **You will become the go-to agent** if you try with all of your power and tools at your fingertips to find the client the home or other real estate investment of their dreams. Make sure you sell to happy clients and list homes which are sold as quickly as possible so you ensure your sellers are happy too.

Becoming the go-to agent is easy if you enjoy what you do. However, if you discover you do not like this business, then it will be tough to establish yourself as the go-to agent. Also, it is important to work with many different clients and within many different realms of this business. If you do discover you have a knack with investors or seem to draw in older couples down-sizing or younger couples buying for the first time, then target this group a little more with your marketing campaigns. For instance, if you are spending time with young couples who are starting to give you some steady streams of referral business, begin to promote yourself to these couples. Place business cards in campus mailboxes if you live near a college, call newly engaged couples you find in the local newspaper, place homes magazines in bridal shops. Whatever you do, reach the market you need to reach while staying in close proximity to all of your other possibilities.

Keeping Your Clients Close

I mentioned earlier how my mother seems to attract clients who are around for the duration. This is not a bad thing and she would not have it any other way. However, for the new real estate agent, there are a few ways you can keep your clients close and your past clients even closer without going to a cooking class or becoming the new best pal of your client. Take a look:

- **Send Christmas cards** every year to current and past clients.

- **Send out birthday cards** to past clients.

- **After the closing, always give a gift to your buyer or seller** as a way to say thank-you and put some thought into what they would enjoy and use.

- **Call up your past clients from time to time just to say hello and do not ask for a referral**. Just show an interest in them and tell them you wanted to just check in. Say hello and then ask about their family, jobs, and interests, and say good-bye. You do not need to ask for a referral because you will get it anyway if you just keep in touch.

There are many ways to keep in touch with your past clients. Find what works best for you. A casino host where I used to play craps will send me an e-mail every couple of months just to say hello. He will ask about my children and my husband and tell me if we are in the area anytime in the future, to let him know because he would love to see us. This host knows me but he has never met my family, yet he will ask about them and call them by name. Even though I am quite sure I am not one of his high rollers or someone he makes an enormous amount of money from when I am in his casino, he still shows great customer service skills by keeping in touch. I appreciate that and your clients will appreciate the little things you do as a real estate agent. Remember your past clients and remember little details about their life. This is the best way to show a client you cared enough to find out about them as people while reassuring them you did not just view them as another paycheck.

IMPORTANT TIPS from chapter seven

1. Positively affirm your best year in real estate will be this one.

2. Love what you do and the money trail will be there.

3. Keep it professional.

4. Learn to market successfully.

5. People do not notice how long you have been in the business, so do not mention that you are a new agent because no one knows and no one will care unless you cannot do your job.

6. Be optimistic and enthusiastic.

7. Do not be a mediocre agent waiting for sales, as long as you are working, go out and work!

chapter eight

Selling Is Your Business— But Can You Sell?

S ales can be tough stuff if you have never been involved in sales before. In fact, even if you have sold things in the past, real estate sales can be entirely different. For starters, you are not selling a thousand dollar piece of furniture, you are a selling a much higher-end item and you are selling a lifestyle. You cannot put a price tag on happiness. Most likely if you try to hard-sell someone into buying a home from you in an area they are unsure of then you are trying to do just that and it can become one of the pitfalls of this business. So, how do you sell real estate? In a word—carefully.

How to Sell Real Estate

In order to sell real estate, you are going to have to master some preliminary skills before you begin to work with a client without offending the client or without appearing to be uninterested in working with them. When working with a buyer for the first time, you need to pre-qualify them before you begin to run around with them all over town. You can do this over the phone if they are insistent upon starting their search for real estate immediately. It is suggested you pre-qualify your clients based on your broker's usual methods. For obvious reasons, I preferred to pre-qualify a client face to face. Anyone can tell you anything over the phone, but it is better to meet potential clients at your office before meeting them at a property.

Buyers will seldom buy from you the first time they work with you unless you are a super sales agent with years of experience. The following list will help you when working with a buyer for the first time.

- **Meet a client you are working with for the first time at the office** if at all possible so you can pre-qualify them for the price range they need to consider.

- **After you meet and decide on a showing itinerary**, start with house number one. Try not to overwhelm your buyer with too many choices. Find out what they want and conduct a search through the MLS to see if any properties will meet the client's needs. See if the client has any homes they want to see which they have found on their own through the homes magazine or by spotting homes marked "for sale."

- **After you arrive at the first home**, unlock the home, hand your clients a listing sheet on the property. Stay with your clients at all times. It is unethical for you to leave a client alone for one minute in someone else's home. The seller likely has jewelry, prescription medication, and other items thieves would want to take should you ever find yourself used as a pawn for this kind of person. It is part of your job to stay with your clients. Plus, you can save yourself problems later if you stay with them in case something does go missing from a seller's home.

- **As you go through the home,** point out its features. For example, if you notice on the listing sheet (or just by looking) that the oven in the kitchen is a self cleaning oven, then if the opportunity presents itself, voice this to your clients. If the satellite dish stays with the home, be sure to mention this. Any appointments which remain with the home should be mentioned as well. Window treatments typically stay with a home, but if this is not the case, point this small detail out. If anything such as appliances or ceiling fans do not stay with the property, mention it as you move from room to room.

- **After you finish the initial showing,** ask the potential buyer if they have any other questions and ask them if they would like to go back through the home. Then, regardless if this is your first or your 20th meeting with your client, do go ahead and ask whether they want to place an offer on the home. The only exception to this is if you are showing numerous homes throughout the day in which case you would wait until all homes have been viewed and then you would ask, "Which house do you want to make an offer on today"? The client will likely tell you they have not decided to do this yet and if they do, this is fine. In fact, it is expected somewhat in this business. However, you need to learn how to move your client to a decision once you have worked with them for a few days on several property showings.

- **Every time you show a house,** do not forget to linger a little longer in areas you know will be important to the buyer. For instance, if you know your client is a car fanatic who collects antique cars and the home has a three-car detached garage, stay a little longer in the garage while making conversation about what the person liked or disliked about the home. Let them get a good feeling of how it would feel to be in the garage working on their older cars. If you are showing a young couple with children a home, linger a little longer in a room perfect for a children's den or stay a while in the fenced in backyard and mention to them what a perfect place for a trampoline and maybe a swimming pool. Paint a picture and then put them in the masterpiece.

After a day out showing property to a potential buyer, take the time to find out what their favorite home was and discover what they liked most about it. Schedule to meet again to look at the property a second time or schedule an appointment for the following day to sit down and discuss writing an offer if you cannot encourage them to put something down on paper right then. Talk to your client about their financing needs. Encourage them to get this process started by getting them interested in going to a bank or mortgage company to begin lining up their financing. Think positive, smile, listen, and ask questions so you will know exactly what your client wants and expects to purchase.

There are some tips for you to use to ensure your success as a real estate agent. Actually, these tips and hints can help you in any sales career and sometimes in daily life. They are designed to help you succeed.

1. **Always be willing to go the extra mile** for your clients but never go for infinity. You have heard the expression, "You give an inch and they take a mile," and this is very true in real estate. Go the extra mile, but refuse to go on a road trip.

2. **As an agent, it may be necessary from time to time t yourself to your clients**. When you are the listing agen give the client a reason to use you as their agent. Tell them what you are going to do for them when they become your client. How are you going to market their home or property? What will make you stand out? Why will you be able to get their property sold? As a buyer's agent, why would buyers prefer to work with you? What can you offer the buyers in search of a home of their own? What makes you most capable of working with these clients?

3. **Have confidence; speak with authority.** Do not be wishy-washy. Speak directly to your clients and give your professional opinion when asked for it.

4. **Learn to be an expert at building rapport with your clients**, beginning with a general concern for their well being in the real estate transaction.

5. **Always be in control and never lose control** of the sale or property showing or in any other real estate transaction. Always be in control of every client-agent situation.

6. **When you meet your clients, look them in the eye and practice the double handshake**. If you pick up on a client who is stand-offish, a handshake will suffice and if you know the person is not one who wants someone in their personal space, back off a bit when you speak with them.

7. **Give reassurance to your client**. Always assure them of the positive features in any transaction. If you are working with buyers, reassure them they will find what they want. If you are working with sellers, reassure them the time the property will be on the market will be minimal. Then keep

ses. Find a buyer what they want and move a
uickly for a seller. In short, go to work and get
e for your clients.

8. **Pay attention to what your clients say to you**. Know their wants and needs in the real estate transaction and then be smart and jot down a mental note to remember everything they said.

Realize You Are Selling a Dream and an Investment

The sooner you realize you are selling a dream and an investment, the sooner you will begin to understand and appreciate the fact that everything happens in real estate on its own time table. If you try to rush any aspect of showing or selling a home, your buyers begin to feel uncomfortable with you and will not buy from you. To sell real estate, you must learn the art of being able to relate to your clients and understand their investment goals. You want to know what their ideas and dreams are for their purchase. If you can, put yourself in their shoes while they explain to you what their wants and needs are. You will be able to sell them their dream.

There is a flip side to this too. If you become so in tune or in touch with what the buyer hopes to accomplish, you may forget what it is you need to accomplish. While you never want your buyer to feel rushed in their decision-making, you also do not want to let them drag their feet. You have heard of the salesman who nods and says "yes" throughout a sale to condition their buyer to saying yes? Believe it or not, it does work in many instances. For example, "Yes, I see what you mean, this is a lovely bathroom."

Or "yes, the kitchen is large and open." Condition yourself to nod your head at the appropriate times and use the word "yes" when appropriate. It works and enthusiasm is contagious. If you are enthusiastic about a home or an investment property, then you will find your buyers will be, too. In fact it makes it easier for you to say at the end of the day, "Yes, I think you have found your home." Still, remember the used-car salesman and do not overdo any of the positive affirmations! There comes a time when everything can be overstated and too many *yeses* are obvious to the person with a background in sales.

Tips for Success in Selling Real Estate

Many million dollar agents will offer you their secrets to success, but be aware that in this business you cannot trust everything you hear. You will always be a competitor for any other real estate agent in the business *in your area*. My brother works with my mother but when I was in the business, my mom and I worked in different offices. Even though she is my mom, we still competed for some of the same business whether we acknowledged it or not. While moms and their children may share their secrets to success, it really would not benefit another agent to make you into a million dollar agent by sharing all of her secrets with you unless she directly benefits from your sales. If you work for a real estate broker who is also a very good salesperson and highly successful in sales, this is another story because they will likely offer you some very good advice which they will benefit from because they make money when you make sales!

In the years I spent in real estate, I only saw one exception to this rule. My office was right across the hall once from a highly successful multi-million dollar producer who broke the real estate mold. She offered advice and seemed to revel in the success of others as much as her own. She is the exception and not the rule, and some of the reading material is suggested here because she encouraged me to read these books. They profoundly influenced my business, almost as much as she did.

Why the Real Estate Sales Agent Must Sell Differently than Anyone Else

We have already established that making real estate sales is tough. We have established that clients will seldom buy after just one showing. What we need to do now is try to understand why this is the case and see what we can do to overcome it.

When I was new in the field, my client was a hairdresser and her husband. He was a used car salesman at the time. They ran me all over town for weeks. The first weekend I went out of town, they bought a house from another real estate agent. Every time I showed them property, they would walk around wearing these silly little grins, and the husband would coach me on how to sell real estate. This man even told me that the reason I was unable to secure a sale with them was because I was the first to speak after I asked them to buy. He said, "In sales, after you go in for the kill (sale), then you ask for the sale and then you shut up." I had been taught this before in sales but did not think it really applied in home sales. However, I was only somewhat right. When you are dealing with other salespeople, this is a tactic that will work because they have been trained to do this and expect to be sold this way. This man was a used car salesman, and they are especially keen on this sales tactic. Some salespeople, like these clients, will be more trouble than they are worth and you need to spot them before you spend too much time with them. Sometimes you can stop them in their tracks by pre-qualifying them especially if you take your time doing this. Even though the lady was my hair dresser and we had bought a car from her husband, they still wasted my time and gas money for days and then bought from another real estate agent. However, we have bought cars since then, but not from him. I guess it cost them more in the long run than it did my couple of tanks of gas.

As a real estate agent, you are going to sell to people from all walks of life and the only way you will ever make it in this business is to become who they want you to be when they are interested in buying property from you. I have been a babysitter, the dog sitter, the banker, the marriage counselor, the parent, and many other roles just to satisfy a couple while carting them around from house to house. Sometimes, it is tough to wear the hat you are supposed to wear. Real estate agents often find they are the negotiator between a couple squabbling over which house to buy or the mediator when one part of the happy couple has enough debt to sink the Titanic without the water. You have to assume the role your clients want you to assume—to a certain extent. However, the more you can keep yourself distant from any emotional attachment to your clients, the better off you will be. You want to be a neutral and professional friend, but if you become too involved it can be harder to sell a home to the buyer.

I love one particular Century 21 commercial with a lady and her real estate agent. The buyer thanks the agent for showing her 20 houses and the agent tells her it is 34 or whatever it was, and the buyer acts surprised. The agent quickly says, "What are a few houses between friends?" If you become too friendly with your buyers, you will find many of these scenarios and you will be putting a ceiling on what you are capable of earning. When it comes to showing homes, 34 houses would be considered far too many to show. However, believe it or not, you will do it. You will do it more than some of the more experienced agents if you do not learn to close in on a deal, ask for the sale, and obtain a written offer to purchase.

"I do not want to become known as the agent who just "sold" a house to a client but I do not want to become the agent who escorts a buyer who does not want to buy a house either. I would like to meet that happy medium of selling a home to a buyer who wants to buy now while never being a pushy agent who gains an apparent sale which the buyer did not want and is likely to fall through at any given moment."

Real Estate Agent Who Wanted to be Left Anonymous

A real estate agent is expected to play the part of the friend/agent. Often, all the client really wants is someone to hold their hand and to tell them it is OK. You should be able to do this successfully, especially when you are holding the hand of a person clutching $300,000 in the other hand!

Many clients expect you to make them feel comfortable. If you are going to achieve success in real estate, you need to be just as comfortable selling to someone who earns $16,000 a year and is interested in buying a home for $20,000 with their life savings as you are selling to someone who wants to buy a $1.2 million estate. If you become overly eager to sell to the millionaire, you may just lose a sale and if you are uninterested in your $20,000 home listing, you will lose that listing.

You have to find a way to be comfortable with people from all walks of life and most million dollar real estate agents recognize this early in their careers. I never had a problem with this but I think it is because I have been everything from rich to broke so I am not easily intimidated or ever impressed by money. However, some agents have a problem with this. Many of your jet-setter real estate agents do not do well with buyers looking to buy a small home and some of your new agents are uncomfortable selling to wealthy clients because they are looking for a multi-million dollar home. There must be a balance if you are going to make it to the top in this business. When you realize the difference it can make in your salary, I am willing to bet you will quickly become accustomed to rubbing shoulders with anyone when you want them to buy from you.

A real estate agent must sell differently with each new client. It is important for agents to be able to match the buyers' personality. If you are at ease with the people who are buying from you, it is easy for you to wind up the end of your day with, "Stan, which house did you like most?" And after he tells you, all you need to say is, "We will go ahead and offer them $140,000 and see if they like the offer." It is comfortable, you are old buddies at this point, and there is nothing too pushy about it—only a team effort approach and a way for you to help your buyer right into the home they want. This is real estate made simple. This is the way real estate sales should be—easy. Best of all, if you have the personality for it, real estate can be just as easy as this. It really can be. It is also a lot more fun this way too!

How to Sell Different Properties

You may find when you start to sell larger homes and commercial properties, often the listing agent is required to be present for you to show your buyer. This is fine for them to be there but do not ever leave your buyer alone with the listing agent. In fact, I would talk to your broker about this before you show the property and as a new agent. You would be wise to take your broker along with you for the showing. Remember, feast or famine and the agents who are feasting are not always doing it because they were so nice to everyone in the business. They have learned to play the game and in some cases, they have learned to play it so well, they have forgotten what it means to play ethically with other real estate agents on the playground. If at all possible, draw up a contract before you go and establish the boundaries between the listing agent and potential selling agent, especially if you are dealing with a multi-million dollar deal. Remember, I was burned once by a shrewd, greedy commercial realtor so I have reason to take precautions and you should trust me on this: take every precaution to protect your own interests!

When showing a property where the listing agent is present, take the lead from the beginning and never let the other real estate agent get the upper hand with *your client*. If you do, there is nothing to prevent the client from going behind your back to deal with the more knowledgeable realtor. Now I know it is beginning to look like paranoia here but do not just read my words on this. Many agents will tell you the name of the game in real estate is to smile, pat the back of your competitor, and then take their last client with a smile and a hand-shake. It is the business and if you are naive, it will happen to you at least once in your career. However, walk into every deal in full control of your transactions and it will be harder for someone to take their best shot at your clients.

There is nothing wrong with securing your position before you meet with the listing agent by having your buyer sign a buyer's agreement, too. Never trust a handshake in this business. A man who made hundreds of thousands of dollars from my father in the cattle business once gave me a one-time showing on a piece of property. I secured the buyer for the property and the only way this man would then agree to sell the property was if it went through another real estate agent with me receiving a small percentage of the sales commission. While the commission still would have been nice, around $8,000, I laughed at the idea and took my client somewhere else. The good ol' boys club never flew very far with me. There is always another piece of property somewhere and if you find yourself up against an unethical real estate agent, take your buyers elsewhere. If they want the property the agent has listed, tread softly with your managing broker in tow!

Sales Techniques

One of the reasons I do not sell anything anymore is because I have sold so much for so long, I am just burned out. I started selling when I was not even able to drive. My parents were appalled when they found out I was going from door to door at age 14 selling Avon so I could save up for a sports car since I knew they had no intentions of buying one. Since my mom was part of the country club scene, my debut as the Avon lady did not thrill her. I can remember going door to door with my little catalog and when anyone told me they could not buy, I would just simply ask "Why?" My career was short-lived once my mother tracked me down but I learned a valuable lesson, and that is to ask "Why?" — always.

If you are not closing the deal, you need to ask yourself why you are not and go back through your approach to see what you missed.

- **First and foremost**, did you pre-qualify your buyers? Can they afford to buy the homes you are showing them?

- **Did you ask** them what they are looking for in a home and then did you show them what it is they want and are looking for in their home purchase?

- **Did you find** out what their "hot buttons" are and did you play on those hot buttons?

- **Did you showcase** the extras of the home? Did you mention the convenience of the location or the privacy of the setting? What did you do to up-sell the home?

- **When you finished** showing the property, did you suggest that you write up the offer to purchase for them? Did you ask for the sale?

If you missed something, then you failed to do your job. You have to be able to do the following before you will ever join the ranks of million dollar agents:

- **Always pre-qualify** your clients; if you do not pre-qualify them, how do you know they are serious buyers who can truly afford the homes they want you to show them?

- **Did you go over all of their lending options** so they could make a decision on approaching a lender to get the loan under way?

- **Did you make a list of their wants and needs** including how many bathrooms they wanted, whether or not they needed a fenced yard, and other amenities? Did you listen to what they wanted you to hear them say?

- **Are you showing your clients homes** they would like to

own and can afford or homes your clients would just like to be able to afford? There is a big difference.

You will learn many sales techniques for dealing with different client types. However, you will eventually become so good at closing real estate deals and securing offers to purchase, you will expect to do it every time you show property. That is when it is safe to say you are evolving into the coveted million dollar agent ready to take on the world of real estate.

IMPORTANT TIPS from chapter eight

1.   Pre-qualify every buyer you ever work with in real estate.

2.   When working with buyers, linger in areas you know will appeal to a buyer. Paint a lovely picture for them of their new home with them in it!

3.   Have confidence and speak with authority.

4.   Remember to build a genuine rapport with your clients.

5.   Reassure your client.

6.   When working with your buyers, go the extra mile with them but bypass the road trip. Look for a way to bring your buyers together with a seller.

7.   Pay attention to your client's needs.

8.   Practice nodding your head in a 'yes' fashion and train your clients to say 'yes' without being obvious you are in 'yes' mode for them to buy!

9.   Secure your position when working with other agents and your buyers.

10.   Always ask "Why?"

chapter nine

Making Plans for Success in Real Estate

The Competition Is Fierce

Competition is fierce in real estate; however, it never needs to affect you and the way you conduct your business. You are probably thinking fierce competition will be a very real part of your daily business life, but that is not so. Here is why. Call it optimism, over confidence or even arrogance, or whatever you want to call it but if you are sure of your abilities to sell and to become successful in this business, others may place themselves in competition with you but you will never view another real estate agent as your competitor because you will not need to.

If you are your own competition, you never need to worry about competing against another real estate agent. You will likely stay out of the inner circles and the back-biting cliques too. If you are a producer, you do not have time for this childishness and if you carry more than 20 listings at any given time and work with only pre-qualified buyers, you do not have time.

Another reason you will not notice or care anything about the fierce competition is because you will be generating the majority of your own leads. Outside of floor calls you take because you want to and not because you have to, you will never be competing for the same business your fellow agents will be biding for. In fact, many of these agents will never even come close to your sales and abilities to close these sales because you are going to be doing what the average real estate agent will not do. You will be willing to work and you will have to work very hard to meet and exceed the goals you are going to set for yourself. However, with the determination to succeed and in keeping your eyes focused on the end result—you will be a star performer!

What will set you apart is not only the fact you will be willing to do the things others will not do but you will be willing to try the things you have been told do not work. You will try them and make them work. Marketing and promotions will become your forte and you will find you are eager to work at promotions to pull them off successfully to gain new business. Lastly, you will not notice the competition as being fierce because you will become the fiercest competition any real estate agent will have—not because you go after their listings or because you try single-handedly to undermine them but because they will envy your success and will want to know how you were able to become so successful in such a short time. They will probably never ask you but will be watching from a distance.

How to Overcome Competition as an Obstacle

The best way to overcome competition as an obstacle is to view it as an opportunity. If you find competing is unavoidable, for example, when you and several agents are being interviewed by homeowners for the listing, consider it as an opportunity to find out how strong your listing presentation really is. If you get the listing; assume it is pretty good but if you do not, take the time to call the client and ask "Why?" in a non-intrusive way. Tell them you are not trying to undermine them or the agent they chose but ask them if they would mind telling you areas of your presentation where you need improvement. Homeowners should not mind providing you with feedback if you explain to them you are new to the business and want to be aware of where you need improvement. Afterwards, thank them for their time and learn from what they had to tell you.

Following is a list of some of the biggest obstacles and objections you will face as a real estate agent and how to overcome them.

- **Many agents** who have been in business for a long time still gain referrals from people they dealt with 20 years ago. They have built a solid and reputable business providing good service consistently enabling them to keep their clients loyal to them. Do not try to win their business because it cannot be won. If an agent has a long list of loyal customers and a number of years in the business, there is no way you can gain this business nor should you try to do so. These older agents with good reputations in business are not the real estate agents you want to cross when you are beginning your new career. Furthermore, there is plenty of business to go around. Go out and find it.

- **Another obstacle** which you will probably hear several times within a month when you are working hard to build your business is the number one excuse people will give you when they do not want to list or buy from you right now. However, it is probably the truth. You will hear, "Oh,

I already know someone who sells real estate." Then they will ask you if you know the person. If you have not heard of them, you will because often a real estate agent will bring their license out of retirement long enough to do a couple of friendly deals for some friends and retire the license again.

- **During your first year** in real estate, you will run up against the obstacle of being a new real estate agent. Being a new agent does not need to be an obstacle, but you do need to decide how you should handle it. Turn the objection into a challenging opportunity. Tell the client all of the reasons they should allow you to serve them and you will likely convince them to give you a chance. Let them know as a new agent you are full of fresh, new ideas. You are dedicated to giving clients the attention they deserve and are committed to putting their best interests first. I know a new agent who claimed to be a new agent for three years and played it to his advantage. He would say, "I am new and I am hungry for the business. I will work harder for you than any other agent." I wonder if he still uses this line now that he is a broker with over ten years' experience.

- **In a large office**, you will be the new kid on the block who will be put to the test by the office losers—those people with great aspirations but no work ethic. Because I am a firm believer in the power of one, I advise you not to be tempted to team up with another real estate agent. Many agents who notice you are doing well and tend to have some fresh ideas would love to think of a team concept. However, a team concept will likely cost you more than you will make. You will end up doing most of the work and they will take half of everything you make. Not much of a deal for you. If you have this so-called opportunity presented to you, thank them for their interest but tell them you prefer to go it alone based on the goals you have set for yourself and your business. I had the opportunity presented to me several times and escaped without teaming up with anyone because I am selfish. I do not want to work hard and hand over any of my money to anyone else. Be selfish and stay solo.

- **Another obstacle** you will need to overcome is in the area of listings. You will go on a listing presentation in the early days of your career and someone will ask you how many listings you have and you will tell them you do not have any and send them into shock. Why would they want to list with you if you do not have any listings of your own? Laugh this off. When you face the obstacle of no listings and you are trying to obtain your first listings, you will probably need to let the seller know you are new to the business and very interested in listing their property. You will need to remind them you will certainly have the time to market and promote their house and offer to do several open houses for them too. In a worst case scenario, offer a shorter listing term to secure the listing. This is called a chicken close but you want the listing and you need it so take it on a trial run if it is the only way you can secure it.

- **Top agents** have something to offer their clients. They have a track record. Since you are new to the business and do not have one yet, bring to the table what you do have. If you have a track record in any other sales, you might mention this because someone who is listing their home with you will be interested in how you plan to generate interest for their home. You must have something to offer the seller and some way to convince them you are someone they want to do business with at this time. Share with them what you plan to do to encourage interest in their home and make sure that if the seller entrusts you with their home to sell, you turn it over quickly with a lightening fast sale!

- **If you choose to join a small office,** you should know one of the obstacles you face will sooner or later become the obvious. Many sellers prefer to list with large offices because they feel a large office with numerous agents will sell their property quicker than a smaller office. Then come marketing and advertising. Some sellers believe smaller offices do not have the availability of funds to advertise their listing effectively. This is really just a myth. Often, as far as exposure goes, a smaller office can draw more attention to a listing than a larger one. However, agents in a larger office tend to work together to help one another sell the listings in the office first before looking outside of the office for other possible choices to show their clients.

Throughout this book we talk about objections and how you can overcome them, but for now it is important for you to understand you need to expect objections and you need to learn how to overcome them quickly.

If you must compete for listings and buyers, then let the Internet do most of the work for you. Hire someone who will set up a Web site for you that enables you to download your new listings and work with your Web designer to find out the way your Web site will be an interactive experience for its visitors and it will give you a cutting edge above your competition. We will discuss ways you can use your Web site to gain business and place you at the forefront of your local market later.

Planning for Success

Successful people plan for success. They do not just set goals; they design a plan to meet those goals. They do not just set high expectations; they put a deadline on their goals and expectations. Once their deadlines are met, then they set new goals and the process starts all over again.

I have worked with all different types of sales people. I have worked with the arrogant closer who makes his clients feel as if they cannot afford the home if they do not buy from him. I have worked with the pathetic closer, the agent who whines about the fact they need to make a sale. You name it and I have seen agents in action waiting for the right opportunity to close in on a deal. Some of these agents know the client does not want the house or piece of property they are showing the client but they do their best to close the deal anyway. This is also known to some as a special circumstances chicken close. There are many ways to close a deal in real estate and you can do it ethically. One such way is to really *sell* the property. You can do this if you have been collecting information about what the client wants in a property. When the time comes for your client to make a decision, you simply ask them to buy. You remind them of what they liked and disliked about the property and you go from there. If you are only showing homes or real estate based on the list of things the buyers have told you they want, sales will come easier for you.

How to Be a Successful Closer

There are many ways to sell a client and knowing this gives you the power to decide how you want to sell your clients. Still, it is better to let a buyer decide they want to buy and better for a seller to want to list than for either one to be coaxed. There are several ways you can be helpful both to a potential seller and a buyer you are working with as your client.

- **First, be ready to write a contract** when your buyer wants to write their contract; otherwise someone else will gladly do it!

- **Make sure you used all of the resources** you had available to help your buyer make an informed decision on all of the properties they wanted to view.

- **As you show your buyer a property**, ask them for feedback to see what they liked or did not like so the next showing date will be full of more "likes" with fewer "dislikes."

- **If your buyer cannot make a decision** between two or three final choices. Find out why. Perhaps the three homes are running together and the client needs to go back through one or two of them so they can look at the options again. Sometimes, it simply means they want further information from you, as their real estate agent. Do what you can to put a new spin on things so the buyer can buy and a seller can sell.

- **If you find a buyer is not buying** because of an affordability issue, you need to stop showing them property at once and talk with them about changing their price range. Do not waste your time showing a client properties they cannot afford because often, even if a lender has a client pre-qualified, there is no way the client wants the payment or the mortgage the lender is willing to give him. Know when it is time to regroup.

- **Whatever obstacles are preventing your buyer** from making an offer to purchase, view them as an opportunity to make a stronger case for a sale and go in for the kill with it. For example, if the garage is too small for your avid car collector but the home is situated on five acres, you might say, "You know, Gary, I noticed that, too, but let me tell you why I thought that might appeal to you." Of course, then you would go into explaining how the yard allows room for a garage expansion and really begin to show the buyer you are in tune with his needs because you can show him how to get everything he wants just by *envisioning* it as already there.

- **Learn to use descriptive language in your sales** when talking with your buyer. For example, describe a kitchen as a spacious country kitchen and back porch as a quiet porch overlooking the most beautiful view of the lake. Paint it up for the buyer so they will see their new home through your eyes as well as their own.

- **Ask for the sale** and expect to get it.

Following are some suggestions to use so the seller will know you are the right agent for their home:

- **Let the seller** ask you questions.

- **Tell the seller** what you will do to try to encourage a quick sale on their property.

- **Offer references of other satisfied clients** who listed their property with you in the last three to six months.

- **Have** open houses.

- **Offer open communication** and let the seller of the property know when they can expect to hear from you each week. Tell them you will call them or e-mail them with feedback after a showing so you both can work together to secure a quick deal on the property.

- **Offer advice on staging the home** so the home seller can make their home more appealing to the potential buyers who view the property.

- **Give a listing of everything you provide** as a listing agent including an estimated time you think their property will be on the market.

- **Do not forget to leave behind a CMA** so the client will have in front of them all the particulars of other sales in their area including the time the properties have spent on the market.

- **Ask for the listing** and expect to get it.

"One of the biggest mistakes a new agent makes with me is they forget to ask me what it is I want. If they want me to buy a lot, they should ask me to buy it. If they want me to list one of my spec houses, they should ask for the listing. If they do not ask for the listing of one of my houses, why would I want to give it to them? If the agent cannot ask me to list one of my houses, they are not going to be able to ask a buyer to buy one of my houses."

Builder who builds multi-million dollar homes along the coast who wanted to remain anonymous

Remember, you have to wine and dine your client before you can go in and expect a relationship. You cannot meet someone at their home, walk in, and say "Hello, sign here." They will show the door to you just as quickly. You have to walk in and meet them, sip a glass of iced tea, and make small talk before a potential seller will show you their home. Then you can go into your listing presentation. Unfortunately, doorstep listings just do not happen often. To obtain a listing, plan to spend some time with your seller.

IMPORTANT TIPS from chapter nine

1. Remember you are your own competition and the only competitor who matters.

2. View all obstacles as opportunities.

3. Being new to real estate is not an objection but an opportunity to show your natural abilities in your career choice.

4. Remember a new agent has new ideas so share some of them with your sellers and buyers.

5. Let your clients know you are dedicated to giving your clients the attention they deserve.

6. Be hungry for the business.

7. Believe in the power of one.

8. Turn your listings quick so others will have confidence in you.

chapter ten

Referrals, Advertising, and Nonsense

Gaining Clients

There are lots of ways to gain new clients—through referrals, advertising, canvassing, calling "for sale by owners," using cold-calling techniques, and through your Web presence. You can gain clients through an agency network typically found through national franchises that have a good relocation department. You can find clients when you are working your business and you are willing to go out and try to find them. Remember, if you are working, the business will come.

The Issue of Referrals

You have probably been told by every other seasoned realtor that referrals are the real estate agent's lifeline. This is only half-true. You do need referrals to gain business and to ensure future job security, but you mainly need referrals because they are simply the easiest way to gain business. Think about it. Referrals are gained through word of mouth. You are not paying a hefty advertising bill to gain the business. You are not out pounding the pavement to get the business, and you are not spending time, effort, and money to make your phone ring. Yes, referrals are a great added benefit to doing your job right. If you do a good job each time you work with a client, referrals will follow. But even if you get to the point where you can work on referrals alone, you do not want to do that. You will want to combine working referrals and doing what we have been discussing throughout this book. Then someone will have to write a book on becoming the $10 million dollar agent, which in all honesty, is achievable.

Referrals are a great way to build your business and to ensure you are doing a good job as an agent. If you are gaining referrals, you are probably leaving a trail of satisfied clients. A true referral is someone who calls you up and says to you, "Margaret told me to call you" or even "I keep hearing your name and I wanted to work with a good real estate agent." You have finally arrived when the stream of referrals seems to be never-ending. You are doing a good job taking care of your clients and you are making a name for yourself along the way.

There is always a way for you to ask for referrals. There are appropriate times throughout your real estate transactions with clients to ask for the referrals of friends and family members, but it is another thing to get them. Furthermore, you will most likely gain the most referrals after the sale rather than immediately following a closing.

If you do a good job and handle each of your real estate transactions professionally, the referrals will soon follow. There are some things you can do to ensure you have a flow of referrals without ever asking for them.

- **Always treat your clients** like they are the only clients in the world.

- **Always be courteous**, considerate, and honest in your real estate dealings.

- **Handle your clients** with professionalism from start to finish.

- **Please the client**. If you are the selling agent, remember the client wants a fast sale for the most amount of money. Do that and you will gain referrals from the client. If you are the agent for a buyer, help the client find the property they want and make sure they are happy with their purchase. If you literally talked them into buying the home and came across as being more interested in the sale than whether they buy what they want, it is safe to say you probably will not gain business from them.

- **Call your buyers** or seller after the closing and ask them how they are doing. Show genuine interest in following up with your clients. Ask if they found everything to be just as they imagined. Ask them if they put up that white picket fence they talked about or made plans for a new roof. Show interest in their happiness with the home.

- **And finally**, add each contact to your mailing list. Remember their birthdays, send Christmas cards, birthday cards, and call them every now and then. You have made a professional friend for life and if you are someone to be trusted in real estate dealings, placing the client first at all times, you will gain the business you want and need.

One thing to make a habit of doing is contacting referrals instantly upon receiving their information. Even if the referral is not going to be interested in doing real estate business for a few months or even a year, contacting them immediately is very important. This way, he or she will not have time to think about finding a real estate agent when the time comes for them to do so because they will already have one! Take a look at the appendix for information on how to contact referrals by phone.

After you begin to call referrals, you will see these calls are the easiest to make. Most of the time, just tossing out a familiar name will ensure you are not met with a phone slammed down in your ear! Sometimes, your call is even expected, making it that much easier to get to know your future client!

Whatever you do, remember to keep confidences. The tough thing about referrals can be the fact that the referred client uses the opportunity to find out what you know about the friend who referred them. Luckily, I have not been put in a compromising situation by a referral that particularly stands out. However, I remember hearing a story once about a man and his wife who referred friends to a realtor friend of mine. He said the entire time he worked with the couple who was referred to him, the woman kept asking questions about the other couple. Two years later she married the man who referred her to this real estate agent and it all made sense when they started shopping for a home together and each put their homes on the market! Always, remember to keep confidences. While it is public record how much a house sold for and will most likely even be placed in your local newspaper, try to avoid answering questions about another client. Remember, think like a professional. Often, innocent remarks or answers to simple questions can be misconstrued, and believe me, it can cost you a lot to open your mouth when memory loss would serve you best!

Advertising and Paying for Clients or Self Promotion

It is an ugly truth about this business. You are going to spend more than you make the first couple of months. In fact, if you can negotiate with your broker to provide things such as business cards, advertising your first few listings and picking up the cost of ads in the homes magazines, you will be better off in the first few months of business. Advertising can be one of those unavoidable things which can run you out of business if you do not watch what you spend. Following are places you need to advertise or things you must have:

- **A must do:** You must advertise in your local area's homes magazine.

- **A must have:** You must have business cards.

- **A must do:** You must place an ad in your local paper about your new affiliation with your broker's firm and you should always advertise your listings.

- **A must have:** You must have an advertising budget in place immediately.

- **A must do:** You must decide where your advertising dollars should be spent.

Outside of these five things, you do not have to do anything else at once in regard to advertising, but I recommended you also do the following:

- **You need** a **Web site**. A Web site may be too expensive to do on the beginning. However, if you refer to my Web site **www.susanalvis.com,** you will see a sample of a site that did not break the bank to build. The Web designer I used is at the bottom of my Web page and I recommend everyone and anyone I can to her because she is fair in price and honest in business. No matter who creates your site, make sure you know how to change your listings and content. I use Network Solutions for my e-mail and Web hosting but you can use whoever you feel will do you the best job. Real estate professionals find a Web presence and placement are essential. Writers can help you do this and so can whoever hosts your site. If you are going to provide Web content on your Web site, hire a writer or write your own content using keywords to improve your Web placement. Using real estate terms frequently in numerous articles you place will help you improve your placement among search engines.

- **If you are going to deal with new home builders**, invest in contractor pencils with your name and phone number on them. They are excellent tools to leave at job sites with the crews building spec homes in your area. Talk to your local hardware store about discounts if you order volume.

- **If you want to specialize in lake property**, use the power of self-promotion. It can be expensive to buy T-shirts and caps but if you want to be the first name people think of in some markets, self-promotion may be necessary. On the lake, the drink cozies for keeping drinks ice cold are ideal. If you want to work with contractors as we mentioned, pencils are great but baseball caps or sun visors are often a big hit too! T-shirts with a catchy phrase or just your logo and name can help you get your name out but they are very pricey. If you want to sell the half million dollar homes on the golf course, have golf towels printed up and leave them at the pro shop or take a moment on a Saturday morning and go hand some out. You have to be creative and if you have the money to self-promote creatively, you will love the results!

As a successful real estate agent, it will be easier for you to self-promote but you may have to wait for your budget to catch up before you begin working your business aggressively. One of the best ways to self-promote is to place car magnets on your car door. An agent in our area has cars already painted with their company logo and name on them. They also have a moving van for their clients to use when they buy a home from them. This is an agent who is queen of self-promotion and she has become so good at selling real estate, she now has buyers' and sellers' agents who work for her. Did she do this all at one time? I doubt it, but she has evolved into a real estate giant. In fact, no one is any bigger than her team in our area. She has also managed to use teams to build a real estate empire—one exception to the team thing we discussed!

Another thing to do for yourself is become known for something through your name or motto or mission statement. I told you about the ERA conference in Phoenix where the National Rookie of the Year became the Rookie of the Year because he promoted himself as the available agent. This agent advertised he was the agent who would answer his phone or call back within an hour 24 hours a day, 7 days a week. It must have worked for him because he sold millions of dollars in real estate during his very first year of being an agent!

In our area, we had a lady who became known as the "Talking House Lady" because she would list her homes and add recordings to be heard via radio transmission when anyone would pull up to the house she had listed—something new at that time—which she used to her advantage to make a name for herself.

If you will take the time to learn how to self-promote, you can spend less money in advertising. Even then, if you are a great negotiator, you will work around those advertising costs with your broker.

Nonsense

You may live in an area where you can advertise your listings on a cable television guide or homes and community announcements channel. If so, and the advertising is cheap, consider it unless there are so many channels that no one will ever see it. Years ago, we had a channel on cable television where agents advertised their listings called Video Marketplace. I spent too much money on it and although I did gain business from it, now I realize I could have done as well with one ad frame as I did by running 10 individual frames. However, one of my good buddies sold the ad spots and I bought from him every time he sold spots for his marketplace. I did gain business from this avenue—just not enough to warrant 10 spots advertising a slew of listings.

My point is this. Everything you do in this business should be done in moderation or you may find yourself in advertising debt. Also, you should remember at all costs, what I told you about budgeting the advertising you do. If you want to advertise, stick to your budget. There will be too many advertising opportunities to mention and if you do not plan ahead for these opportunities, you will be blindsided when you hear about a good deal. Never *buy now*. Always tell your ad reps you will *never buy now* but take their rate sheet and consider their rates and advertising for a later date. Many of the ad sales reps are good at convincing clients to buy from them immediately because of upcoming rate changes. This is a chicken close and rarely occurs. If in doubt, try turning down a rep and calling them back in two weeks and see how quick they are ready to write up your sale. If not, thank them for their time and they will be back with an exception especially for you before you can say "advertising." It is just the nature of their business.

Television is a good tool for agents to use but I must say for real estate agents in most areas radio advertising will do little to help you. Why? Because your audience cannot see you and they cannot put a name with a face. Also, they cannot see what listings you have even if you tell them. If you are going to use radio to advertise, do it as a talk show. Find an AM station to give you air time once a week or every couple of weeks to talk about the real estate market in your area and then plug your business as the go-to real estate business to deal with in the area. If you want to make good use of radio, do it in a way to gain the most clients. In other words, talk about your business and offer sound advice instead of running a 30-second ad someone can miss if they so much as scan the radio. You decide what is most effective for you when you advertise.

TV Infomercials

I had an agent call me the other day and ask me what I thought about TV infomercials in general. She was thinking about doing something locally in the format of a television infomercial. If you read my book, *How to Buy Real Estate without a Down Payment in*

Any Market, you know I am a believer in infomercials because I first learned about the no-money-down concept thanks to Carlton Sheets and his famous infomercials. If you are going to use television in your area and can afford to do the infomercial format, you should, but I do not have any statistics or war stories to share with you at this time. I can offer this suggestion: if you choose to do local infomercials, try to include some of your active listings on any new subdivisions or condominium developments you are representing. In fact, if you are going to do an infomercial, go out and visit housing developments *before* you record the infomercial and mention to the home builders what you are doing. Who knows, you may be able to gain some listings out of your new project that would more than pay for the cost of the infomercials if you watch what you are doing! Another suggestion would be for you to watch other infomercials, even on a national level and find out what seems to be working for other agents. If you can catch a name and city of the agent, look them up on the Internet and e-mail them to ask how infomercials worked for them or better yet, call them. Always learn from other full-time professional agents in other areas. They may give you an idea of something you can use in your own local area.

In regards to infomercials and real estate talk radio shows, keep in mind that there are several approaches for using these mediums. First, you can plug your listings and yourself, or offer a Q&A format, or simply an ongoing infomercial like the one Carlton Sheets has done. Put some time in planning what will work best for you and your area. If you are going to air an infomercial, seek out past clients who will go on the air as a testimonial for you while offering a recommendation to others to consider you as their credible real estate agent. Find out what has worked best for others in the past and incorporate those things, too. There have also been successful stories of infomercials in the same format as the original Carlton Sheets infomercials. They are worth your consideration if you incorporate what you see on his original infomercials and appeal to your local audience.

Let Us Talk About the Virtual World

The Internet has changed the way everyone does business. It has given people the opportunity to see more, learn more, and do more than ever before. It is important for agents to use it and to have computer skills. Even if you have been selling homes for 30 years, you are now in need of certain skills if you are going to be successful. Fortunately, community colleges and adult education classes are offered for adult students to learn how to work successfully within the virtual world. If you do not know how to do simple things online, sign up for computer classes ASAP.

Some realtors believe that if their broker has a Web site, they don't need their own site. That is a judgment call of course. However, consider this. My brother is very computer savvy and the Internet has opened doors for him. Considering he spends a certain amount of time every week ensuring he has high Web placement among the search engines, it is safe to say, it works. I have never known him to waste time when it comes to business.

As a new agent, take a look at the Web sites of other agents in your area to see what they are doing and do it better. Conduct a search online for top producers in other areas and go to their Web sites. Look at what they do and use some of their ideas combined with your own to make your Web site the best it can be. Here are some ideas for your site:

- **First, you need to have a bio page that tells your clients who you are and what areas you work**. If you want to include any educational background, feel free to do this too. Include any designations you have such as your CRS or GRI.

- **Then you need to include your current listings**. The person who designs your Web site should be able to show you how to upload your listings to your site since they will change frequently.

- **Any relocation information you feel is important to people who are moving into the area** should be included on your site such as a list of public and private schools, area hospitals, and businesses. Include the job outlook for the area and top employers. You may even want to include links to the area Chamber and hotels in the area.

- **Remember, one of the more important aspects of your Web site** will be to gain the best Web placement possible for search engines. Whoever builds your Web site will know how to guide you on this, but try to think of keywords that would be used to search for a real estate agent in your area. In addition to those keywords, you will need articles written either by a professional or by someone who can produce well written articles to encourage better placement among the search engines. The articles need to include scattered keywords strategically written to give your site the exposure you need. You can do this yourself but you will gain better placement in the long run if you hire a writer with technical skills in SEO (search engine optimizations).

- **Always be sure to include the basics**—your name, contact numbers, company logo, affiliations, and a mission statement if you have one or a slogan.

- **It is a good idea to provide a link** to search the available listings in the area and not just your listings, if possible. However, make sure you have a bold statement on several pages of the Web site stating you can show any property listed within the MLS. You may also add something like, "Contact me for information on listings that may not be listed on this Web site currently."

Keep your Web site interesting and encourage e-mails from people who will be searching for a home soon. If you want to add the guestbook feature, incorporate a place for the person visiting your Web site to include their phone number and mailing address if they want. Any lead you get through your Web site should be worked immediately because if a person is looking at real estate sites, the first person to contact on a follow-up is usually the agent to win the business.

When you are dealing with Internet leads you gain from your Web site, you should have an auto-responder set up to answer your e-mails informally when you are away from your computer. A good letter sample is in the appendix. However, the auto-responder is not meant to take the place of good, personalized service. After you get the lead and the auto-responder has been sent, you should still follow up with a phone call or an e-mail to initiate further contact on your next business day.

We have talked about things you should do and even a thing or two you should not do as a new agent. However, if you want to earn the business of others, you need to be willing to act quickly when you receive a lead. Know what to do with the leads you receive and if you have planned carefully, your office should already be set up to take the leads you get and run with them.

IMPORTANT TIPS from chapter ten

1. Work your business effectively and consistently and the business will be there.

2. Referrals are the cheapest way to earn business.

3. Take care of your business and your business will generate more clients for you.

4. Consider starting your business with an effective Web site and learn how to maintain it for best possible traffic.

5. Establish an advertising budget and think twice about any advertising you do.

6. Never BUY NOW when buying advertising.

chapter eleven

Becoming the Number One Agent in Your Area

Becoming the go-to agent in your area really starts with the belief you can become the go-to agent in your area. If you do not think you can succeed, you are right! Believing in your own talents is half the battle. People will tell you real estate is a dead-end career choice. It is a dead-end career choice for the agents who do daily luncheons, party on the weekends with the inner circles of real estate, and care more about property tour and social hour than they do about returning phone calls and canvassing for new business. However, if you are dedicated and driven to succeed, you may find something different altogether. You may find a career worth having and a life worth living.

Becoming a Top Agent

We have already determined anyone can become a real estate agent. We know it takes more effort to become one of the top agents in any given area, and it requires even more effort to stay on top once you reach the top of your game. You can never slow down: quitting is not an option. Many top producers are never satisfied to sell a couple of million dollars in real estate after they have sold $10 million dollars worth. Who could blame them?

While the climb to the top is never easy, once you get there, enjoy it. Savor the fact you are at the top of your profession, but do not get lazy if you have a tendency to meet your goals and then just revel in that excitement alone. Remember, "You are only as good as your last sale."

In real estate, you are only as good as your previous year as a real estate agent. You and everyone else will start over at the end of the year. You will realize this most if you are on a graduated scale of commission, based on your yearly performance with your broker. January 1 usually marks the beginning of another year in sales. You will work hard all year long and your broker will appear in your doorway to let you know what a good job you did and to remind you that all of your sales contracts dated after January 1st will start over on a 50/50 split. They will tell you not to worry about it though because with your abilities, you will be back at the 80/20 in no time, and that is when a good dose of reality will set in.

As a new agent, your broker will probably tell you how much you sold the previous year and then they will tell you how much money you made when they hand you your 1099. They may tell you what educational requirements you will need to fill in the coming year, and they will let you know if you are up for any awards within your local real estate association. Most area real estate associations will recognize their top producers as million dollar producers and multi-million dollar producers to the community either through congratulations in the newspaper or on a television commercial. Make sure you do not miss your chance to become recognized as a new agent who reached these achievements.

After your first year in real estate, you can see what you would have done differently if given the chance. You can also determine what your new goals are. As a new agent, you will be given plenty of opportunities to reassess your career as you go along and most brokers will take the time to coach you along the way. However, you need to be self-motivated and driven to succeed all on your own. So, let us go ahead and see where you need to focus.

Top Agents Know How to List Real Estate

I loved being a listing agent. Maybe it was because I never had the patience to look at numerous houses with the buyer who just could not decide between their top ten choices or maybe it was just because I liked the idea of having many listings hard at work for me at any given time. Whatever it was, I was a good listing agent and I liked the fact that at any given time contracts could come flying in with my name all over them to present. It was a thrilling highlight of my real estate career.

As I sat down to write this chapter, I tried to think about the most number of listings I ever had at one time. It was when I worked for a local franchise of ERA Real Estate. I had several new home builders listing exclusively with me, a couple of condominium complexes where I was the primary listing agent for the newly constructed units, and a world of scattered independent listings. It seemed as though I had any listing I wanted.

I remember feeling married to my business during that time, even though I had a personal assistant who handled many duties for me, there was never enough time to do anything fun. Life was just all about work. The assistant worked taking listing pictures, organizing budgets, and handling client calls. She worked 30 hours a week as hard as she could and could never catch up with the work. It was fun and stressful, but the money was good and at that time in my life, my husband and I really needed it.

I remember an investor who worked with me waiting over an hour to see me and when he finally came into my office, he was livid. He informed me that I was driven by greed and that unless I got it together and sold his listing by the end of the week, he would pull his listing and never list or buy anything else from me again. I had forgotten to return his call. Not once, not twice, but multiple times. All I could say was that I forgot and apologize. I was alienating an investor I had worked with almost since day one.

Something in his eyes told me I had better start selling his house or he really would pull his contacts, listings, and keep his word about never buying from me again. I got busy and called everyone I knew and even added a bonus out of my own commission to the house. Keep in mind, this is not recommended if it can be avoided but this was a client who had basically helped rocket my business in the beginning. Both he and his wife had multiple contacts and they sent me a huge amount of business. I could not afford to lose them as clients especially since I was considered a new agent. His house sold. He forgave me and went on later to buy many properties from me.

At the beginning of this book, I told you about an outspoken investor who had a knack for putting me in my place. After my ordeal with him that almost ended my business dealings with him he told me, "Susan, I was not mad that I had to wait an hour to see you. In fact, I was even proud of you for being so busy, but I was mad because you had forgotten those of us who helped you out along the way, and I was mad when I opened up the homes magazine and saw all of the junk you are listing. You can have many listings, but if you get to the point where you are listing junk, it will work you to death and never really pay off for you. You will lose the customers who matter to you and your business just because you want the most listings in a book." Reality in large doses seems to be hard to swallow, but this man always told me the truth and taught me a great deal about real estate.

As a new agent, you must return your phone calls, handle your customers with care, and make them feel that they are your only client every time you deal with them. Everyone wants individual attention. They want to matter to you and if they get the feeling they do not, they can take their business down the street or worse, down the hall to another real estate agent in your own office.

He also taught me something even more important. Listing junk is worse than listing a bunch of over-priced homes and vacant land. You will work yourself to death and never see a commission. You will lose your good customers because you waste too much time trying to find a buyer for property that cannot be sold for the price you have on it.

That year, I remember my goal was to always have the most listings. I think I accomplished that goal. An agent had told me the secret to success was to list everything you can because when anything is pulled up in the MLS, chances are listings will be shown daily that belong to you. And that did happen, but for every listing I had, there was work to move it. It is the agent's responsibility to the seller to sell the property, but taking on an overpriced listing that will be hard to sell just does not make good business sense.

After months of being one of the top listing agents in our office, I remember deciding to set up a checklist for listing properties. My assistant and I sat down and formed a checklist to decide which listings to list and which ones to refer to someone else. The following list is criteria we began to use.

- **List properties within a 30-mile radius of the office.** I was notorious for listing properties an hour or more away from the office because my dad was in farming and had contacts he could send me. Unfortunately, buyers in our area wanted farms in our area. Often the farms I listed were out of the area where buyers I worked with wanted to buy. After we decided to stay within a 30-mile radius, we saved time and accomplished more.

- **Do not list over-priced properties.** You have heard the old adage "they wanted something for nothing," and this holds true for sellers who are not willing to make their property worth their asking price. They want big money but have no intention of improving the property. There is one exception to this. If you are going to list over-priced properties, make sure you talk the seller into owner-financing or providing a lease option on the property. Remember, if you later face an appraisal, an over-priced property may not carry the appraisal you and the potential buyer will need to secure financing on the property.

- **Do not criticize properties in areas you do not want to work.** The property might sell quickly if the right buyer comes along. However, if it is located in an area you do not want to work at all, what is the point in listing it? I worked with an investor of rooming houses once and it was hard enough to get a client interested in looking at the properties let alone psyching myself up to go and show them the houses. If I had not been fond of my clients/ sellers, I would not have taken on the listings.

- **Do not take a listing if you are going to be on a deadline of 60 days or less to sell it.** You will not have time to promote it and the money you spend to advertise the property will never be earned back through the sale of the property. I knew several realtors who only listed properties for at least six months. Explain to your seller it is a formality and you have no interest in keeping the listing unsold for that long but if you are going to list a property to sell, you will accumulate some advertising fees and want the listing to remain yours for a set number of days.

- **Be ethical in your business dealings and avoid taking a listing that belonged to another agent in your office.** Even if an agent in your office has a listing pulled and handed to you or if the listing expires and you end up with it, sour grapes will still be there. Do not do it. It is more trouble than it is worth and you will eventually have problems with the listing due because of sour grapes or the fact that you cannot sell the listing, either. Also keep in mind that when a listing is pulled from one agent and given to another agent in the same office, the same exposure remains. Unless the new agent is just a lot better at moving their own listings, chances are the property will not move any faster.

A quick note on the last statement: if you have a client who comes to you and lets you know they are pulling a listing from another agent in your office and will be listing the property with you, ask them not to do it. Tell them you will try your best to help the other agent move the property and explain you will be unable to take the listing, regardless of what your office policy is. Make it *your policy* not to take the listings of other agents in your office.

The client will respect you for it and so will the other agent who will probably hear about it from the client.

As I mentioned above, I loved being a listing agent. If I had it to do over again and pulled my license out of retirement, I would probably just list as much as possible and avoid buyers as much as possible. However, let me tell you why that is not really possible in the real world. Many people will call you to show your own listings. What are you going to do? Turn them away? Of course not. It looks better for you if you list, show, and sell your own listings. However, you can list more if you remain busy with your own listings more than actively seeking buyers. Be fair warned, though, if you try to become a listing agent only and avoid promoting yourself to buyers, your bottom line will be greatly affected unless you are an astounding listing agent.

It does make sense that most agents would prefer to list rather than work with buyers. Today everyone is concerned with rising gas prices, so working with buyers can be very expensive, and you will spend more time with buyers than with sellers. The more listings you have, the more you have properties out there within the MLS waiting to be shown. If these listings are shown and then sold, you get a commission for listing the property and if all you did was list the property, you have earned a commission without having to do the work yourself. You are letting the property do the work for you and that is a nice way to work the business. Remember, the more quality listings you have, the more money you make and the flip side is the more unqualified listings you have, the more money and time you are losing. Get the good listings and then get them into the MLS quickly and onto your Web site even quicker.

Top Agents Know How to Close the Deal with a Buyer

As a new agent you will be happy to drive around a buyer for days on end as they look for a home and you have your first live one on the line. However, remember the idea is to close the deal with a buyer so you can earn your commission and they can find a home they like. Following are some tips to use to ensure you are able to get your buyer the home they want, earn the commission you deserve, and move onto buyer number two!

- **Remember, top agents always pre-qualify their buyers.** You think it will never happen to you but it will. A young couple all starry-eyed and easily impressed with their life and their savings for a home will stroll into your office. They will proudly announce they do not owe anyone anything and they have a savings for a home. You will know they are sincere buyers ready to pull out the checkbook. They have dreamed of owning a home; they have taken the necessary steps to ensure they can afford one, pay a sizeable down payment, and secure financing. Just as you pull out a sheet of paper to take some notes, the lovely young couple in front of you will hand you a list of 20 or so homes and the page numbers of a Homes Magazine so you can easily find the home they want to see. You open the book and notice that house number one is $350,000 followed by 19 more in the same price range. The couple seems content with their choices of what they can afford so you ask them to follow you to the first house you know to be vacant and you explain you will call for an appointment on the way. Once you arrive and you begin to make conversation with the couple as you go from room to room, you discover some interesting points. Point number one is that only one of them even has a job and point number two is that the one who is working makes $8 an hour at a local restaurant. Wow, how did you end up here showing the district attorney's house to these two? Remember, pre-qualify your buyers and you save them embarrassment and yourself some time.

- **After you pre-qualify your buyer**, use the worksheet in the appendix to find out more about what the buyer wants. I suggest giving this worksheet to all parties involved in the purchase so you can get a good feel for what each person wants in their dream property. Have your buyers fill out the worksheet alone if possible and then study it before you line up properties to show them. See if you can search the MLS for the properties that seem to fit your buyers best. If you know you are considering showing a property which is not suited for the buyer, do not show it. It will only cloud their judgment and make it harder for you to get the buyer to put in an offer to purchase. I suggest showing a pre-qualified buyer who is ready to buy, at minimum, three to five homes. Try to stay with the three-to-five-rule and see if you can close a buyer within these parameters.

- **If you are an agent who uses the worksheet** your buyers take the time to fill out, you will be able to save yourself time when you begin to search active listings to show your buyer. You can also pick up the phone and call top agents in the area and tell them you have a pre-qualified buyer looking for specific things in a home and ask them to let you know if they get a listing that will meet the needs of your buyer.

- **If you are working with a pre-qualified buyer**, at some point you need to ask them if they already have someone in the banking business they are working with and if so, you should suggest they visit the person. Also, always listen for any cues there may be financial things to work out and if you are asked what to do about certain things, give your unbiased opinion and send them straight to a loan officer who is better equipped to help buyers prepare their financing.

- **As an agent working with a buyer,** you want to use the worksheet your buyers filled out to help you find the right property for them best and to help you find their hot spot. The worksheet in the appendix will help you find out what it is that your buyers will not be able to resist in a home of their own. It will give you an idea of the monthly payment they find comfortable and it will give you a general idea of their expectations for their home purchase. You should make every effort to accommodate your buyer's needs and you should keep the worksheet for future reference.

- **Remember, if you are an active listener**, you will discover what it takes to close a deal with one of your buyers. Listen to what you are being told and use it later to help you play on those hot buttons and close your deals. For example, if you know the buyer wants four bedrooms and a Jacuzzi tub in the master bath and the home has these features, you will want to mention the home has everything they want and it is at a realistic price.

- **Often, when it comes right down to closing the deal**, it will come down to price, regardless of what you are told initially. It is amazing but even if a buyer is pre-qualified for $150,000 and they start out looking at the $150,000 homes, they may end up looking at $100,000 homes and amazed that you did not show the home at $100,000 when it clearly is exactly what they want.

To sell real estate to buyers with the cash to take the deal to a closing table, you must learn how to sell. Learn to reaffirm the hot buttons of the buyer. Learn to listen to the buyer's ever-changing wants and needs. Learn how ask for the offer to purchase. You may eventually have the buyer who will never buy because you do not ask for the sale or you may find you have a buyer who will never buy from you because they like traveling around with you from home to home looking at property. These people may never buy and if they do, it may not be from you. After all, you are their chummy friend and somewhere along the way, you lost your purpose of working with them and you wind up empty handed.

If you are going to be a successful top agent who can move real estate, you must keep it simple, keep it professional, and work your business quickly. When it gets right down to it, people want to be shown what they will want to buy. Find it as soon as you can for them and save yourself and your clients precious time.

Top Agents Work for a Living

We have covered what you need to do to be successful in your business. One thing you need to realize is that consistency pays. If you are consistent and diligent in your efforts to earn a good living in real estate, you probably will make it in this industry. However, if you give up the desire to be successful, you will fail. You have to work hard every day you go into the office and if you do, the rewards will be mind-boggling.

I have an aunt who was always being on the go. She had children about my age, who later became real estate agents, and I was around them growing up. Whenever I saw them she seemed to be on the move. She would have to stop what she was doing to look something up for someone or she would be talking about her business at family gatherings and I was so impressed by her success. My aunt and uncle both were successful in the business. They worked their business and were persistent. They knew if they did not work, someone else would soon have their business.

Something to keep in mind throughout your career is that you are dependent on your own sales. You are ultimately responsible for your own successes and failures. If you do not sell property, you do not earn a commission check. The reason this business is "feast or famine" is because people who choose real estate as a career often are relying on their income from real estate to support their families. These people, more than anyone else in the business, need success in the business and need to take care of their clients, but you would be amazed at how many of them do not.

You may not realize it until the real estate office down the hall is suddenly empty, but every day new real estate agents go broke or agents throw in the towel and new agents rush on the scene. The agents who stick around are those who are able to earn a good income from their own efforts. That is the key to a successful career in this business. You need to know you will earn money only from your own efforts. If you do not earn the income you want, it is only because you did not work. Get out there in the community and work to become recognized, do the things other agents are too lazy to do, and you will be a success. Not only will you be a success, you will be a GREAT success!

Top Agents Take Advantage of Every Opportunity

As an agent, you will have numerous opportunities to take advantage of every opportunity for advancement. In the business of real estate, what that means is to take advantage of investment opportunities. The only way you can obtain a pay raise in real estate is to sell more real estate or start buying some of your own.

Top agents know it is important to get ahead by taking advantage of every opportunity presented to them. Take a look at some typical ways real estate agents can advance their incomes.

1. **Leases and lease management.** If your company does not have a rental agency or lease office, you should take it upon yourself to become the go-to person within your office for leases and lease management. While you may not want to do this solely for your income, you should talk to your broker about handling leases. There are two ways to approach it. The first is to handle only the leases you are personally offered through clients and referrals. The second is to talk to your broker about handling your own leases as well as those that come in through the office or through relocation. If you decide to do this, you would need an office within the realty business, and you would need to offer other agents some sort of commission or referral fee if they referred a client to you. Leasing is big business and you can even specialize if you want. You can handle general leasing or you can handle commercial leases or stick with large developments and only work those. I recommend doing it all if you are going to do it. The leases

you secure can mean an extra couple of hundred dollars for you *per lease* per month. Furthermore, in a business where you must sell to earn your income, leases ensure you have an income when you do not sell.

2. **Buying fixer-uppers to turn quickly.** Buying run down properties to fix up and turn around for a quick sale is another way successful agents turn ordinary careers into extraordinary incomes. Even if you do not like the idea of tool belts, hammers, or paint, you can fix up homes and turn them into cash in your pocket. You have to be patient and make it a habit to find properties you can fix up and re-sell and naturally, you want to do your research so you are sure to buy properties that will make money very quickly. If you are going to fix up a home and re-sell it and you have to have a mortgage on the property, you should be able to fix it up and hold onto it based on your income. As a new agent, fixer-uppers may not be the way to go from the beginning, but at some point you need to become involved in buying and selling handyman specials. There is money to be made on them.

3. **Buying investment properties to rent.** If you are going to become a million dollar agent, sooner or later you will need to begin building your own portfolio of investment properties. When the stock market is volatile, the best investments remain in real estate. I used to find it funny that so many wealthy people would dump hundreds of thousands of dollars into the stock market and never even take a look at real estate investments. To me, it just did not make sense. There are thousands of stocks on the market and millions of acres worldwide. However, there appear to be new introductions to the big board all the time. IPOs

are making headlines but there is not any more land to be made. Why are smart investors not investing where there is always going to be a demand with less and less supply? If you are an active real estate agent, you are in a unique position to take advantage of one good deal after another. Take a look at the investments you want to own and start building your portfolio.

4. **Buying land at a bargain to develop later.** I had a friend who used to go around and buy up lake properties. He often paid too much for them but nonetheless, he bought property after property on the lake. He bought many of them on no-money-down terms. The great thing I discovered by watching him was that he eventually controlled the market to a certain extent. He was buying all of this lake property in a particular area and once he appeared to buy all he could buy, he drove up the prices and started selling. In the area where he lived, he could do this easily because the property on the lake was expensive anyway (as it is in most areas). Still, he was able to control his market and he made a fortune. Somewhere along the way, he began to buy vacant land. I thought it was a somewhat risky venture for him because he did not have the equipment to develop property or even the knowledge of how to do it. However, he knew people who did. He put up the money and as far as I know, they only had their labor and expertise invested in the property. The partnership was a success, and the men profited in a big way from the venture. As a real estate agent you will have many opportunities throughout your career to cash in on cheap investment properties, handyman specials, apartment complexes, and other opportunities. If you learn to take advantage of every opportunity, you may find buying

vacant land, when it is a real bargain, can help you make a handsome profit too. Always keep in touch with your real estate contacts. Developers and home builders are often in a position financially to need a partner and if you have the land and they have the expertise for developing it, you can make a nice chunk of change.

5. **Taking Options.** Since taking options can often cross all sorts of lines ethically and legally, we are not going to discuss taking options in great detail. However, you need to know as a real estate agent, you can find many opportunities to take an option on a property and cash in at the appropriate time. Taking options is simple. Basically how it works is someone will approach you about listing their home or piece of property. They will tell you they want a certain amount for the property, for example, $50,000. You discover they could get a lot more. You will tell them it is worth $100,000, but they do not care; they just want a quick sale and $50,000. You will take an option, making you a partner in a sense, for $1,000 on $50,000. A deadline will be put on the option and if you do not sell the property by the time the deadline expires, then you will lose your $1,000. However, in a best case scenario, you will sell the property and you will pay the property owner his $50,000 and keep the rest. Options are a great way to earn extra income on the properties you are selling but you must check with your broker to find out what his or her policies are on the subject of options.

Recently, I watched a television special about properties that are considered unmarketable because of notorious crimes committed on a particular property. Properties where notorious crimes took place were showcased. The home where the Manson murders took place, Nicole Simpson's condo, and other homes were discussed. Properties damaged by the crimes that took place in them are hurt in value for a short time. However, after watching the show, I became aware that this is only for a short time. For instance, this show announced that the family of Nicole Simpson sold her home for over $200,000 shortly after her murder. However, later the condominium brought over $1 million and regained its place among valuable real estate.

If you are going to buy property damaged by crime, be sure you can hold onto it long enough for the stigma of the crime to wear off. In our area recently, a similar opportunity came up. My brother called me all excited about a 1,200-square-foot home that was available for sealed bidding. He explained the bidding minimum was around $37,000 and he went on to say he thought $42,000 would buy it. He said, "Susan I will send you some comps. Houses in the area sell for around $129,000 and up. This is a great deal." The first thing I wanted to know, of course, was if it was such a great deal, why would $42,000 buy a 1,200-square-foot home? "Well, it needs to be completely gutted," he said, "and you will need to do work on the inside, and there is more." As he said it, I joined in, "Someone died there." In fact, a very brutal murder had taken place in the house. I told him I would think about it and get back to him.

My husband and I had watched the television special on investment properties ruined by crimes just weeks before so I was not concerned about the stigma lasting forever on the property. However, I was concerned about the fact it would not sell quickly so I knew if we bid on the property and our bid was accepted, we would need to fix it up and then rent it for awhile. Anyway, I missed the bid deadline and never even went to see the house. However, a few days later, a friend of mine was at my house and she let me know that she had indeed, looked at the property. She and her husband flip many properties and she's done really well with handyman specials. She said, "It was in bad shape. It needed to be gutted. Evidently, the murders that took place there were brutal and when someone went in to hide the evidence where the murders took place, they did not try to cover it up." From the blood stained walls to the hardwood floors with evidence too, there would have been constant reminders of what happened there while you were fixing up the house. This is why the bid was at $37,000 to open and $20,000 to fix it up would have been about what this property would need. However, you never know, with work and determination, the right investor could have made around $70,000 on the property if they had the time to wait for the right buyer and could stand to be in the home until all of the reminders of what happened there were gone.

Real estate agents who list such properties for sale do have to reveal that a crime took place in the home, and while the stigma can be never-ending, most damaged real estate can have some high margins for profit.

Become the Rookie of the Year

You know what to do to become very successful in the real estate business. How far are you willing to go? In your first year of real estate, you should realize certain things. First of all, your office, if part of a national franchise, will likely have members who will attend a national conference. You will want to go and you will want to be recognized as a highly successful rookie your first year in the business. Why is this so important? First of all, in this business there are too many agents bidding for the same business. While there is enough business to go around, remember, a great number of agents do very little business and a small handful take over most of the business. If you want to be taken seriously in this business, you will need to become a player. To be taken seriously, you need some credentials attached to your name.

One of the best credentials you can have is Rookie of the Year. Whether the award you win is in your large office or in your professional affiliation in your local area does not make a difference, but if the recognition is given somewhere, you need it so you can use it for your self-promotion. If you are part of a national franchise, talk to your broker about what awards and recognition are given out each year at their national conference and find out what it will take to become recognized.

If my memory serves me well, the Rookie of the Year I told you about at ERAs conference with such impressive numbers sold $10 million his first year in real estate. He was widely recognized throughout the conference and even taught a seminar on what he was doing to gain so much business. I liked his enthusiasm.

Moreover, he seemed to be a master of the art of self-promotion. He became known in his local area as the real estate agent who always answered his phone any time—day or night. However, since most people value their sleep, other agents did not see why this was important. He pointed out it was a marketing tool more than anything else. Seldom, if ever, did he have a midnight caller and rarely did his phone ring before 7:30 in the morning. Still, his buyers and sellers liked to know he was available to them and so he made sure to answer his phone all the time.

Whatever you do, develop something people will remember about you. I worked with a super lady in real estate by the name of Robin Hood. Her name, of course, was recognized throughout the real estate community and widely through our general area. I thought it was great when she put a cap with a feather in her rear window of her Mercedes. She used her name for name recognition but she also provided great customer service with a great degree of professionalism making her widely known and respected in our area.

Find a motto or develop a mission statement and then use it wherever you go. Become the "real estate agent always available" or your "community-oriented real estate agent" or the "real estate lady with the moving van." Find it and use it. Your career is depending on you becoming recognized and it can very well be what sets you apart!

IMPORTANT TIPS from chapter eleven

1. Even after you reach the top, you can never slow down and you can never quit.

2. As a buyer's agent, you are only as good as your last sale.

3. As a listing agent, you are only as good as your last listing.

4. You must be self-motivated.

5. Consistency pays.

6. Be diligent in your efforts.

7. Never lose the desire to succeed in your real estate business.

8. Buy investment properties and take every opportunity to fix up homes and flip them quickly for profit.

9. Become the Rookie of the Year in your franchise organization.

10. Always be a multi-million dollar producer.

chapter twelve

The Internet Agent

Having a Web site and a professional Web presence are important. Becoming Internet savvy will allow you to gain new clients while offering you many tools to use throughout your career. You will find tools to use in your daily business activities and best of all; you will gain contacts who will help you build future business relationships.

Getting Started with the Whole Web Thing

When you make your decision to become a real estate agent, you need a Web site. It is important jump in with both feet and have someone build your Web site. You can check online for someone to create one for you. One of the best on the Internet for interactive Web sites can be found through Barbara Carneiro at **www.barbaracarneiro.com.** She is easy to work with and not as expensive as some of the other designers. Best of all, she teaches her clients what they need to do to gain better Web placement.

Search Engine Optimization (SEO) and Page Rank

If you are going to hire someone to build your Web site, you will want the world to see it, and the only way to do that is to gain better page rankings among search engines. There are many ebooks out on the subject of SEO and gaining better page rankings. After you build your Web site, you want it in the top 10 ranks among Google and other search engines. If a client is looking for an agent in your location, you want to make sure you are one of the first Web sites to pop up so you stand a fair shot at their business. Clients will not know about you if they cannot find you so you need to have some knowledge on how to have the best page rank or placement among the search engines.

Using META tags, keywords, and copywriting services can ensure a better placement. Should you choose to hire a Web designer who offers placement services, you will be able to learn about driving your ranking upward among Google, Yahoo!, and other search engines. This is different than pay-per-click. In the pay-per-click scenarios, you will pay each time someone clicks on your link on the search engines and this can get expensive. Plus, the more you are willing to pay for each click, the better Web placement you will realize. While there is nothing wrong with the PPC route, you will gain far more exposure in the long run if you work to improve your overall page ranking.

Link exchanges can help increase your page rankings too. Building partnerships through link exchanges can ensure higher Web placement but you want to take the time to create good partnerships just as you would in any other aspect of your business. As an agent, you should probably stick with link exchanges through a network of real estate agents. Be careful about link exchanges with sites that appear to be agent-oriented but hold no affiliation with any well-known agency or real estate affiliation. They often are affiliate sites and could drive traffic you do not want and even initiate spam in some cases.

So why go to all of this trouble? For the money! The Internet has become a powerful source for agents to gain new leads. Relocation is often handled by clients rather than companies and very often a client moving to a particular area will go ahead and arrange their own real estate agents now using the Internet. Gaining new leads through the power of the Internet is a great way to automate your business and if you have the right software and auto-responders, you can run your Web site practically on auto-pilot after you take the preliminary steps to set up your Web site and ensure great Web visibility.

Online Tools and Ideas to Use

You will quickly discover all sorts of neat marketing tools to use on the Internet. For instance, as a new agent setting up your Web site, your Web designer will probably tell you about the tools to drive more traffic to your site such as the Google keyword tool. It will show you the keywords you should use on your site so the search engines will pick it up and your page ranking will improve. The keyword tool is used those who write Web content for the Internet—a technical way of writing for the Internet. A good content writer can fill your Web site with real estate-oriented pages to ensure your Web page remains in the top three positions, based on research for best placement among the search engines.

As a new agent, you do need to network with as many agents as possible throughout the country so you can have contacts who will keep you in mind should they have a client moving to your area. This is easy to do if you work with a broker who is part of a large franchised organization. However, if you work for a small real estate firm, you will need to get out there and network with as many people as you can—through your Internet connections.

One thing you should do is take a look at the Yahoo! groups online. Approach them for posting your links to your Web site on the real estate oriented sites. These groups are also great places to find ideas and network with agents from all over the country. Choose your group wisely and do not opt in to receive e-mail because your e-mail box will be flooded. Do join these groups so you can post your links and use a heading such as "Real Estate Agent in Tennessee Pays Top Referral Fees" and yours will be the name your fellow agents will see when they need to find an agent in your area to refer a client.

Software Programs You Will Want to Know About

There are so many software programs today that it is impossible to sort through the best programs and decide on one to use. One of the best agent-friendly software programs for using an online database is Top Producer and it can help agents manage their database easily and effectively. Further, it has been around for some time, so many of the computer-savvy agents in your office may be familiar with it.

You are going to be very busy with your day-to-day business activities and, therefore, it is important for you to do everything you can to keep your business as simple as possible. Realtor Soft also has products for accounting and agents. Decide what you want to do and conduct a Google search to find the software to accommodate your needs.

The Tech-Savvy Agent

Real estate is so different today than it was even 10 years ago; an agent must take the time to pursue the world of technology. In the Tri-Cities Area of Tennessee, one agent in particular stands out, Scott Eads of RE/MAX RESULTS, who has made it his business to keep up with advancements in technology while remaining up-to-date with designations and furthering his real estate credentials. He offered our readers sound advice when interviewed. In the following pages you will find our question and answer session.

Scott Eads

Susan: *Scott, How long have you been in real estate?*

Scott E: *Five years.*

Susan: *What goals did you set for yourself in your first year of being a real estate agent?*

Scott: *To sell as much part-time as the national average for agents working full time.*

Susan: *How are you able to achieve those goals?*

Scott: *By focusing on technology and furthering my real estate knowledge and education.*

Susan: *What are your latest goals?*

Scott: *To form a team and increase my production through technology. To build my Web site and optimize it for search engines for better Web presence.*

Susan: *What are some of the techniques you plan to use to help you reach those goals?*

Scott: *Increase my education in all areas and to obtain more professional designations.*

Susan: *Explain your normal workday.*

Scott: *Sunup to sundown and beyond.*

Susan: *What do you think are the most important aspects to selling real estate?*

Scott: *Helping people reach their dream of home ownership.*

Susan: *What do you think it takes to become a million dollar real estate agent?*

Scott: *Hard work, patience, and a sincere desire to help others.*

Susan: *Can you tell me what you do personally that has enabled you to become a million dollar real estate agent?*

Scott: *Focus on education, changing trends, and technologies.*

Susan: *What would be the best piece of advice you could offer someone who wants to work at becoming a million dollar agent in their first year?*

Scott: *Get to work and educate yourself.*

Feel free to visit Scott's Web site to stay informed about Tri Cities Real Estate and other pertinent local information and events.

Scott Eads, Affiliate Broker

RE/MAX Results, MAX SERVICE TEAM
4260 Fort Henry Drive Suite 10, Kingsport, TN 37663
Direct: 423-817-1839
Office: 423-239-8121 / 423-477-7355
Toll Free: 800-239-8121
Fax: 423-239-7766
Personal Office & Fax number: 423-477-8863
E-Mail: scotteads@Re/Max.net
Web Sites: www.tnvarealestate.com
www.scotteads.com
www.scotteads.net
www.maxserviceteam.net

IMPORTANT TIPS from chapter twelve

1. Hire a Web designer and get started in the world of Internet marketing.

2. Have a Web designer discuss the specifics with you on how you can gain Web placement.

3. Take part in link exchanges.

4. Know your software and get the software you need to become most effective as an agent.

5. Use Web articles and SEO content for maximum optimization and Web placement.

chapter thirteen

Career and Family: The Real Estate Balance

At the beginning of my real estate career, I could not do it. I never could balance a successful real estate career with my family life and that is why my time spent in the trenches was for only four short years. So it may seem odd that I would even attempt to write about it, but I wanted to show you how it can be done. I watched from the side-lines as other real estate agents successfully managed their careers and their family life. However, I missed ball games and tea parties and all sorts of things while my children were young. Even though my husband had a job with a steady income, I had to work to help support our family.

My brother has a baby now and I have watched and wondered if he will ever fall victim to the business and so far, he seems to have everything in perspective. However, if you would ask my mother if she missed out on many good times with her family uninterrupted by the business, she would have to answer "yes" because it is the nature of the business if you are any good at it.

For me, if I was at the top of my game, selling and listing houses like crazy, I was a horrible homemaker and not at all an attentive mom. If I was all domestic and the soccer mom of the season, my sales suffered and so did my income. There was absolutely no happy medium. I am very competitive so if I was not one of the top agents in the office, it drove me crazy and I would go on a binge listing, selling, and working 16 hour days. Then I would feel guilty and stay home more and try that for a while as debt started to accumulate without my income so I would go after business fighting fires again. It was maddening and that became the reason I left the throes of the business. You see, if I could not be on top, I did not want it at all and I wanted my family more than the business.

However, about the time I decided to leave, I met an agent who had three children of his own and a wife who did not work. He seemed to be thriving in the business and keeping a steady pace. I asked him his secret to success. He said, "I work every other weekend and refer out the business I get on the weekends. I do not work past 7 p.m. because I am at the office by 9 a.m., and I like the way I am doing things, and it works for me. More important, it works for my family." It is still working for him because he is still in the business and is still consistently a multi-million dollar producer.

For the agents who truly love this business, there is a way to reach a happy medium, and I know it can be done because I have friends who are doing it. However, you will have to set some office hours and schedule time off because if you do not, your life is continually interrupted.

Family First

You have heard it all of your life. God first, family second, and career third. If you are not going to go in that order, then family still needs to be first or second. I am not going to get all preachy on you but read *The Power of Positive Thinking* by Norman Vincent Peale and you will realize that is the only order to follow. However, on this earth, family must come first. If you put your family first, everything else should fall in line.

You hear it all the time in real estate. Someone will tell you they got into the business and it consumed their every waking hour. And it does. They will tell you they did not have time for their families and they ultimately divorced their spouse because of the business. And that happens too. However, it does not have to be that way for everyone. If you can get a good grip on your business from the start, you can actually have it all and you can have a good life because of real estate or in spite of it, however you choose to look at it.

The way to balance career and family in real estate is the way anyone else balances career and family. You have a career and you have a family and you keep them separate as much as possible. If you feel as though you are working all the time, you should consider moving your office outside your home so when you go home, you are home. If you have a private office at the office, do not even list your home number on your business cards. Have a cell phone number with voice mail listed and your office number and that is it. I know agents who list their pager number, I was one of them for a long time, and it is just a bad idea. If you choose to have a pager, give the number to your family members and your office with instructions not to give it out. If someone needs you, let your office make a judgment call and decide if it is important enough to page you in the middle of your son's graduation.

Even if you want to be the million dollar agent, do not be *too* available. Even if you are turning many properties, there will always be one or two chatty clients who want to be the center of your world while you are working with them. You will make them happy with a purchase and along will come another client wanting your undivided attention and you will lose sight of what is important.

Selling real estate does not have to take over your life. At the beginning of this book, I told you it was important to make up a schedule you wanted and stick to it for a year. The reason is so you will become used to working the hours you want, and your clients will become accustomed to your office hours. Do not worry about it if you lose one or two clients who do not want a structured real estate agent with office hours, also known as banker's hours. If you are offering world-class service to your clients, it will not matter that you only work 45 hours a week instead of 70 and it will not matter that you work regular hours. Those clients will adjust so they can work with a good agent.

Family is important and if you do not put them first, someone else might and then what have you worked for? If you have children, you may have just worked yourself into a position to start paying child support because this business is very trying for spouses.

Career After Everything Else—Really!

As an agent of real estate, you are in a really unique position. Not only can you set your own hours, you can have a life full of fun if you plan for it. You can take off for a month at a time and if you are successful, you can go to places you never thought you could afford to visit. You can buy an expensive home if that is what you want or drive an expensive car—without the car payment. There are agents earning over $250,000 a year and believe me, they enjoy better life than doctors or lawyers because they are not tied down to their careers, unless of course, they choose to be.

These agents have learned to focus on what is important. They spend their time living out their dreams and when they work, they work extraordinarily hard so they can live an exciting life on the money they earn. They do not let the business tie them down. They set their goals and when they meet or exceed them, they can kick up their heels for a while.

I sat in on a seminar once where speaker seemed to have it together. Keep in mind, many speakers earn $10,000 per speaking engagement and he definitely earned that much or more. He explained to us that he took six weeks off per year. Two weeks out of the year was what he referred to as "me" time where he went out of town alone or with friends. He might take a week in the spring and a week's vacation later in the fall. Two weeks out of the year was "family" vacation time and two weeks out of the year, he took his wife on a vacation. Even though he traveled a lot as a speaker, he knew how to keep a happy and healthy balance for himself and the relationships he valued.

Have you ever heard anyone say, "I love my career, and my family just is not that important to me"? Probably not. However, many times your actions will show those sentiments. As a real estate agent you need to reach the point where you can say, "I love my family, and my career just is not that important to me." If you make the most out of this career choice, you can put your family at the center of your life.

The Balance of the Successful Agent

It is wonderful when you do not have any particular place to be, the kids are off at the movies, there is no laundry to be done or dirty dishes in the sink? It is great to just have time to breathe. As a real estate agent who is going after business, you will not see many days full of free time unless you schedule them. You have to schedule your time off or free time just as you would in any other career.

My husband is a workaholic. He really is. He will never know what it is like to have true free time because he cannot and he knows it. However, one of these days, he will wish he had taken the time to have more fun in life. I know so many real estate agents just like him. I told you, I was one of them. In a way, my mother is a workaholic because unless she is doing something with or for clients, she is not doing anything. Most real estate agents are workaholics because they choose to be married to their work. Believe it or not, if you are a workaholic, it is by choice and not necessity. Here is why.

Physically and mentally you can only give to your business so much. After you reach that point, you are not productive. You will forget to do things you should have done. You will not be able to maintain a personality people will like (because you are tired) and you will lose things and that is just the beginning. Do you know why some athletes get hurt in some of their games? It is not always because of circumstances; often it is because they are overworked and their bodies are tired. Do you know the majority of people who lose money in a casino do so after one in the morning? Because their ability to reason left them at ten! Think about it. Golfers who love the game cannot shoot a good game of golf when they are tired. You cannot be a quick thinker with a bubbly personality if you are tired and overworked, so why do it? If you are not any more productive working yourself to the bone, why not take a break?

I cannot stress to you enough the importance of working on a schedule and advertising your office hours. If you know you have a tendency to overwork, try your best to keep things in perspective, remember your "why." Did you get into the business to become an overworked and rapidly aging workaholic or did you get into the business for more free time? Remember what your goals are. If you do not have children to raise or a family to nurture, perhaps you can pay your dues and work becomes you at this point in your life. However, learn how to breathe and you will find life is more enjoyable.

More Advice

As mentioned earlier in the book, I explained to you why teaming up with another agent can be more to the advantage of the weaker, unproductive agent than to the agent who can make the team a success. However, if you can find an agent who will work with you enabling you both to take some time off, you may have a workable partnership of sorts. Teaming up with an agent, in this case, does not mean joining forces to become a real estate power team. What I want you to do is to find a teammate within your office who will cover for you when you are out of town, sick, or just cannot work all of your referrals and leads. In turn, you need to make yourself available to the other agent for the same.

This works great for two new agents who are just starting out around the same time. There is no friendly competition brewing because you both are essentially starting at the same point with the same focus. You both want to build your business. First, you need to draw up some sort of formal agreement that you both sign in front of a witness or a notary. Agree on a certain percentage should a sale occur when one of you is working the client of the other one. I worked my referrals differently throughout my career.

The best way to work with a teammate you are not "teaming" up with permanently is as follows and this is based on the assumption that the other agent is only covering for you occasionally and you cover for her on occasion:

- **If the other agent takes your floor time**, there is no referral fee. The lead is their lead just like it would be if you picked up an extra floor shift.

- **If you refer the agent a client you have never worked**, they pay you 20 percent of their commission.

- **If the agent is covering you with a client you gained through a referral**, then you split the commission 50/50. Many agents would not do this. However, I viewed my referrals as the golden eggs. I knew if I gained a client through a referral, they would buy from me or if they contacted me about a listing, I knew I would get the listing. Therefore, the lead came into the office because of my efforts so if someone wanted a sure thing, they could pick up the lead but I wanted half. You should too.

- **Should you need to go out of town and you have a scheduled closing** and your broker cannot go, pay the agent $50-$100 for going to the closing for you. Paying an agent a percentage of your sale to just show up for a closing you have already planned for is crazy. Just pay them for their time, and that is it.

- **Remember, whatever you decide to agree upon as far as terms go,** the pendulum swings both ways so be fair to the other agent, and you will be fair with yourself as well.

As you begin your real estate career, remember to focus on the important things. Make time for your family and yourself. Keep true to your goals and your dreams and do not let anyone ever discourage you. Then, you will be successful in all that you do!

IMPORTANT TIPS from chapter thirteen

1. Family comes first.

2. Read: *The Power of Positive Thinking* by Norman Vincent Peale.

3. Do not be too available to your clients because you need alone time with your family.

4. Use voice mail and remember answering phone calls on holidays from clients is simply crazy. Enjoy Thanksgiving, Christmas, and Easter because any client calling you on these days is not a client you want anyway.

5. Take scheduled time off.

6. Learn to relax and breathe!

7. Only team up with another agent for coverage and then return the favor when the other agent needs coverage for their business.

chapter fourteen

The Million Dollar Agent

There are many different factors determining whether you will become a million dollar real estate agent. Other factors determine whether you have what it takes to become a multi-million dollar producer. This chapter will show you what it takes to have a spectacular career in real estate.

The keys to success in real estate are simple if you follow some of the guidelines in this book, but it comes down to whether you are willing to do what it takes to realize success.

Listing Property and How to Do it

Some top agents believe if you are not listing at least 15 new properties each month, you are not rising to your full potential in real estate. However, nothing could be further from the truth if you are in a market where there are not many homes but there is an abundance of real estate agents or if you work in a high-end market with multi-million dollar homes and properties. Still, there are markets where listing a large number of properties each month is possible, particularly if you are in a large office in a large city. If it is possible to do, you need to learn how to do it effectively.

The biggest challenge for some agents as listing agents often presents itself when agents first go out on their initial listing appointment. Even though they have a great personality, a charming corner office overlooking the bay, and real estate know-how, they simply do not know what homes, land, or anything else is worth. In fact, they will be lucky to convey how much they paid for the pen they use to write up the listing agreement much less strike an agreement on what the seller should list his or her home for on the market. This can be avoided if the agent listing the property takes the initiative to find out what a property is worth and more importantly, has a CMA (comparative market analysis) to back it up.

There are several things you should take into consideration when you go out on a listing appointment. The first and most important is how much other homes in the area have sold for and what the current listing prices are on the homes in the area. Using the tools your broker has given you to compare properties and using what you learn from office training and other real estate training, you should be familiar with market comparisons and be able to analyze the home you wish to list. Coming up with a fair market value for the home and conveying the home's value to the sellers will be crucial when you step into a listing appointment and then, guess what? The sellers may want a lot more than you tell them the home is worth or worse, they may need to realize more from the sale of the home because they owe too much on it.

Naturally, most sellers will want more for their property than they can realistically obtain but it is your job to tell them what their home or land is worth and then show documented evidence as to why you feel the way you do. If you have a sound CMA, you will have the proof you need to support your pricing method. If not, the seller may feel as though you just pulled a number out of your hat and lose confidence in your abilities. In dealing with your sellers, handle them and their properties professionally and always go to the listing appointment prepared with a CMA.

Listing Residential Properties

Residential sellers only want to know three things when you go out to meet with them on a listing appointment. They may ask you numerous questions but ultimately, they only really want to know three things. First, can you sell their home and secondly, if so, for how much? Finally, how long will it take you to move it? That is pretty much it. If you can approach listing appointments with the ability to convince your seller to sell through you it will be because you convince them of the following:

- **Yes**, you can sell their home.

- **You can sell their home** for a price they probably already had in mind anyway and with supportive market comparisons, they believe in you all the more because your price and their price were close enough.

- **The seller liked** the number of days or weeks you told them it would take for you to sell it.

Now, here is the tricky part. Sellers will want you to commit to a time when you expect the property to be sold, and you want a listing for at least four months, preferably six, but you just told the seller you can sell it in five weeks or maybe less. Now what? First of all, as a listing agent it is important never to promise a seller the property will be sold in a specific length of time unless you already have a buyer waiting to purchase the property and even then, it is really not good business to make a promise you cannot keep. Do not promote false hope but instead give the seller a time that is realistic. Use the market comparisons to let a seller know how long homes have been on the market in the past in that area.

It really is not hard to please a seller who wants to sell through you if you practice great customer service and do not give false hope or outlandish expectations. The following list contains a few more suggestions to help you make your sellers happy.

- Always return phone calls.

- Offer a fair commission for selling their home (usually 6 percent on residential).

- Give your seller weekly updates.

- Advertise the property and actively market it whether it is through advertisements or open houses.

- Fax or e-mail feedback after a showing on the client's home.

- Pay attention to the seller's questions and give them direct answers.

- Tell them what to expect from their agent and then meet their expectations or better yet, exceed them.

- Sell their home or property; they hired you to sell it so make sure you get it sold!

Another thing a seller wants from their agent is for the agent to present them with good offers. This is not always possible. As an agent, you may present your seller with insulting offers. Not only will a real estate agent write a ridiculously low offer on a property but they will proceed to ask for everything but the seller's first born child. It happens and you cannot do anything about it because you have a duty to present each and every offer you get on the seller's property.

If you are presenting your seller with poor offers, do not offend your seller. Tell them you are obligated to present the offer and know it is not what they had in mind but still encourage them to counter the offer. A good agent knows no matter how bad the initial offer to purchase is, a counter and then another offer can sometimes result in a sale. Remember, sales mean cash for the agents, otherwise known as a payday!

Do not be the agent who is so focused on becoming buddies with their sellers that you forget real estate is your bread and butter. Never present an offer as a dead-end and explain it until you obtain a counter from your seller even if they go back to full price. Keep in mind, without a counter, the buyer often becomes uninterested in the property and this is why so many deals die. Keep the negotiations alive so you can realize a solid contract.

Working with Buyers

Buyers can be the lifeline for many new real estate agents, and seasoned realtors also find their niche working with buyers. When working with buyers, the million dollar agents know they must keep a professional relationship. As discussed previously, the idea is to bring buyer and seller together and not find another friend for life who is not in any hurry to buy. In real estate, it is your job to bring buyers and sellers together quickly and if you are doing your job as an active listener when you are working with your buyers, finding the best deal for your clients should be easy for you if not second nature.

There are several things you can do to ensure your buyers find what they want in a timely fashion and ensure they enjoyed working with you as their real estate agent. First, you should always meet with them to pre-qualify them for the price range of the home they want. Second, it is important to listen to your buyer's needs. Where do they want to buy? What school district do they need? How many bedrooms and bathrooms do they want? Do they want a large yard? Do they need a garage? Knowing what your clients want will save your buyers time and help you realize a commission much sooner than if you just hop in the car and start showing them everything there is on the market.

Follow these tips when you work with buyers:

1. **Listen** to what the client wants in a property.

2. **Ask** your client how soon they plan to buy.

3. **Suggest** they begin to line up financing.

4. **Help** your client narrow down their choices by providing them with CMA reports of the homes in the areas where they have looked so they can realize what the re-sale value would be.

5. **Help** your buyer come together with a seller by learning how to write sales contracts that are accepted by the sellers of the property your client wants to buy.

There is nothing worse in a real estate transaction than for an agent to sabotage their own deal just because they want to ask for too much or show their client their keen ability to work a savvy deal. Often if a client allows an agent to step in and begin to ask for too much from a seller, the deal will fall through. As an agent, the idea is for you to write winning offers when you are working with your buyers and you simply cannot do it if you do not let the buyers tell you what they want. If you see something you want to mention, such as clear termite problems or clear need for a new roof, you should mention it but avoid asking for the Oriental rug in the den just because it suits the room.

"I went into mortgage banking because I grew tired of working with other real estate agents who sabotaged their own deals. They were their own worst enemy. If I could advise a new agent on anything at all it would be for agents to write contracts they know the other agent has a chance of working out for your buyer and their seller. Why waste your time or your buyer's time writing up offers which will never be viewed as a legitimate offer to purchase? It does not make sense for agents to do this because there is time wasted that could have been used to write a good offer."

Retired Real Estate Agent in Nashville, Tennessee

Bringing Buyers and Sellers Together

Learning to bring buyers and sellers together quickly and easily can be the lifeline of your business. Often, you will work both sides of a deal as a mere facilitator of the transaction, and other times you will handle one side or the other. Whenever you find yourself in the middle of negotiations, it is important not to lose sight of your goal to bring the buyer and seller together. Do this effectively over and over again so you can ensure you have a long and profitable career as a real estate agent.

Often in real estate it can be tempting to write creative contracts especially when you have a clear vision of what the seller hopes to gain from the sale of the property. If you know what is owed on the property or anything about the property, it can be tempting to use this information when negotiations begin. Still, as a real estate agent, remember what the CMA shows you and your buyer. What is the fair market value and what is it you think the seller will want to sell for and what is it your buyer will be willing to pay? Find that magic number and hope for the best. Negotiations can be fun until you have one that kills a deal.

As a real estate agent, remember that your goal is to sell real estate when you are working with buyers or sellers. When working with sellers, you must convince them that your ideas for marketing and promoting their property at a fair price which will entice buyers to buy. When working with buyers, you must create a comfortable environment for the buyer to want to buy the property from you. If you are going to be bringing buyers and sellers together, be likeable.

Working in the Luxury Housing Market

According to *The Wall Street Journal*, June 3, 2006, the luxury housing market continues to rise even though less than 2 percent of homes in the United States are worth more than $3 million dollars. As a real estate agent, if you have the good fortune to fall into a market where homes bring in excess of $3 million, consider yourself lucky. It just does not happen in every corner of the market.

It does not necessarily take a gifted agent to sell homes in the high-end marketplace, but it does require more from the agent, and rightfully so. Buyers of these homes have discriminating tastes and even if they do not, they can be savvy when it comes time to pulling out the checkbook or obtaining financing. What this means is that you should take every step to ensure you know everything there is to know about the property but never become in awe of the property or the people buying these higher end homes. It can be the death of a salesman—again.

The million dollar agent appears to treat all clients equally being as unimpressed with the $5 million dollar client as they are with the $15,000 land sale. There is a difference in the commission but remember that all your clients want the same thing. Give dependable, exceptional customer service, and the sales in any market will be there. You must know how to handle discriminating buyers without being giddy and unable to do your job.

In the luxury housing market, there is a piece of advice you will need to remember or it will come back to haunt you. It is this: do not become consumed with the commission you are going to make on the sale. You can bet the buyers of a multi-million dollar home do not care that you are going to make a four-year salary from one deal. They are only concerned with whether the property works for them. It is your job to show them it does but become anxious and someone else will be singing all the way to the bank.

If you have reason to suspect the buyer cannot afford the home they want to see, ask your broker how to handle them. You can never be too careful when dealing with multi-million dollar properties. Less than 2 percent of the population can afford these homes so make sure you have a client who falls in that small group.

Commercial Property

The million dollar agent eventually discovers there is money to be made in commercial property but do yourself a favor and learn how to sell and list commercial property before tackling it. There are so many facets to commercial real estate that a new agent will not have their opportunity for quite some time. Still, an agent who wants to learn the ins and outs of commercial real estate should pursue it but pursue it when they know commercial real estate. There are zoning issues and many other factors which can make a simple deal turn complicated overnight. This is why it is worth it to the agent to check into commercial designations such as the CCIM (Certified Commercial Investment Member) so he or she can be recognized as an expert in the area of commercial real estate. With very few real estate agents nationwide with the CCIM designation, it is one designation new agents with goals and anticipations of becoming a million dollar agent should keep in mind.

It Is Your Turn

Real estate agents are in a unique position to cash in on real estate. There are opportunities all the time for them to acquire property. Foreclosures and other opportunities present themselves in many different ways to the real estate agent and very often an agent will know about a new property ready to hit the market before anyone else will. Agents have their shot at options and other unique offerings and cashing in on any or all of these can be possible. In fact, no other profession allows for inside knowledge on how to purchase a property with little or no money down like being a real estate agent, but you have to know how to capitalize on those opportunities.

One thing to remember when you run across investment properties is to offer the property to any potential buyer you are working with first. If you are going to flip properties and work in the investment end of the business, you need to practice handling your own investments as ethically as possible. This means showing the property to the buyers you are working with without throwing in, "If you do not buy it, I will" because a client will resent your tactic. Make sure if a property comes available that meets your needs and the needs of the client, you are fair and give the client time to reach a decision about buying it. If they do not buy it within a reasonable time, you may make your own offer to purchase.

IMPORTANT TIPS from chapter fourteen

1. Know how to compile a CMA.

2. Return all phone calls and keep your sellers well informed.

3. Bring buyers and sellers together by writing winning contracts for purchase.

4. When dealing in high-end luxury homes and commercial properties, do not even look at the money (or calculate your commission). Just go ahead and sell the property, I promise the money will be there when the deal is done.

5. Use CMAs with buyers as well as sellers so your buyers can see what the market comparisons are for the homes they are considering buying.

6. Begin to accumulate your own properties but never compete with a client for a good deal you are considering; offer it to your client first.

Conclusion

I hope you have enjoyed reading this Atlantic Publishing book and find it useful in your real estate career. It was written to give any ambitious real estate agent an edge when they venture out into the world of real estate. My hope is you will someday refer to what we have discussed and remember where you found your source of information and perhaps drop us a line to let us know this book made a difference. Atlantic Publishing offers a solid line of real estate books. Check out their titles whenever you have the opportunity and read everything you can on your career because knowledge can lead to a great fortune.

I hope you will refer to this book and use the suggestions to inspire your career. I wish you great success as a real estate agent and genuinely hope you become the go-to agent in your area. In conclusion, I leave you with the words of one of the largest real estate investors in the world. Donald Trump once said, "As long as you are going to be thinking anyway; think big." Until next time, live well, think large, and make a fortune because you do deserve it.

Bibliography

1. Eldred, Gary W., *The Beginners Guide to Real Estate Investing*, John Wiley and Sons, 2004 332.63'24-dc22. ISBN 0-471-64711-X.

2. Gitomer, Jeffrey, *Little Red Book of Selling*, Bard Press, 2004. HF5438.25 G58 2004 658.85-dc22. ISBN 1-885167-60-1.

3. Keller, Gary, *The Millionaire Real Estate Agent*, Rellek Publishing Partners, 2004. ISBN 0-07-144404-1

4. Zeller, Dirk, *Your First Year in Real Estate*, Prima Publishing, 2001. ISBN 0-7615-3412-1.

Appendix A

Suggested Reading

Web Sites Worth Viewing

Phone Scripts for the Million Dollar Agent

Worksheets

Suggested Reading for Successful People

1. Dale Carnegie's *How to Win Friends and Influence People*

I wish I had been given this book on day one of starting my real estate career. I needed it. In fact, everyone I know going into a career dealing with people needs this book.

2. Dale Carnegie's *How to Stop Worrying and Start Living*

Another Carnegie book worth your time to help you in your business and in your life.

3. Jeffery Gitomer's *Little Red Book of Selling*

If you want to be a success in real estate, you really must have this book! It is a light, humorous book with many strong selling points for the real estate agent who plans to be a selling powerhouse. Buy it before you begin your career and read it frequently throughout your career!

4. Norman Vincent Peale's *The Power of Positive Thinking*

I have decided I am going to read this book at the beginning of every year. It helped me in my real estate career Use it for your life's map and it will change your life!

Web Sites Worth Viewing

There are many real estate related Web sites worthy of your attention. While there is no way to catch all of them, this list was compiled to help you find some of the more popular sites on the Web today. Keep in mind, this is an ever-changing world and occasionally, you may be re-directed or you may even find that a site is no longer there.

State Associations for Realtors

1. www.alabamarealtors.com

2. www.realtorsofalaska.com

3. www.aaronline.com

4. www.arkansasrealtors.com

5. www.car.org

6. www.colorrealtor.org

7. www.ctrealtor.com

8. www.delawarerealtor.com

9. www.gwcar.org

10. www.planetrealtor.com

11. www.garealtor.com

12. www.hawaiirealtors.com

13. www.idahorealtors.com

14. www.illinoisrealtor.com

15. www.indianarealtors.com

16. www.ia.living.net

17. www.kansasrealtor.com

18. www.kar.com

19. www.larealtors.org/members/default.asp

20. www.mainerealtors.com

21. www.mdrealtor.org

22. www.ma.living.net

23. www.mirealtors.com

24. www.mn.living.net

25. www.ms.living.net

26. www.mo.living.net

27. www.mtmar.com/public_html/index.html

28. www.nebraskarealtors.com

29. www.nvrealtors.org

30. www.nhar.com

31. www.njar.com

32. www.nm.living.net

33. www.nysar.com

34. www.realtor.org

35. www.nd.living.net

36. www.ohiorealtors.com

37. www.oklahomaassociationofrealtors.com

38. www.or.realtorplace.com

39. www.parealtor.org

40. www.riliving.com

41. www.screaltors.com

42. www.sdrealtor.org

43. www.tarnet.org

44. www.tar.org

45. www.utahrealtors.com

46. www.vtrealtor.com

47. www.varealtor.com/index.asp

48. www.warealtor.com

49. www.wvrealtors.com

50. www.wra.org

51. www.wy.living.net

Other Real Estate-Related Web Sites of Interest

The National Association of Realtors can be found at **www.nar.realtor.com**

The International Real Estate Real Estate Digest can be found at **www.ired.com**

For information on VA loans, check out **www.va.gov**

Bank of America always has helpful information for agents at **www.bankofamerica.com**

Homes for sale and so much more can be found at **www.realtor.com**

Real Estate advice and homes for sale can be found at **www.homeseekers.com**

Everyone likes **www.homes.com** and is a good resource for agents and their clients

New agents should become acquainted with **www.fsbo.com**

Other Web Sites of Interest to Real Estate Agents

www.census.gov

www.usacitylink.com

www.virtualrelocation.com

www.dataquick.com

www.propertyview.com

www.ftc.gov

www.creditinfocenter.com

www.myfico.com

www.creditscoring.com

www.hsh.com

www.moneyWeb.com

www.interest.com

www.lexis.com

www.nolo.com

www.statefarm.com

www.fanniemae.com

www.stoprentingnow.com

www.ourfamilyplace.com

www.mortgagewizard.com

www.hometime.com

www.ashi.com

www.creia.com

Phone Scripts

Below you will find phone scripts for you to use when making cold calls, calling FSBO sellers listed in the paper and other scripts.

CALLING "FOR SALE BY OWNERS"

YOU: Hello. My name is Susan Alvis and I am with XYZ Real Estate. I saw your home listed in the paper and wanted to give you a call to see if I could set up an appointment with you to give you a free market analysis. Could I get your first name please?

HOMEOWNER: Why? I am selling my home by myself. I am Bob, by the way.

YOU: Yes, I understand. However, I would love the opportunity to work with you and show you how you can make your home more marketable to potential buyers as well as give you a free market analysis. Bob, you are under no obligation to me, I would just like to offer this free service to you.

HOMEOWNER: Why would you want to give this service to me for free?

YOU: I will be up front with you. It is tough selling for sale by owner but I really would like to help you by offering you some tools to use as you pursue selling for sale by owner. If you choose at a later date to list your property with an agent, I hope you will remember me but if not, my service is still free because it is what I do best.

HOMEOWNER: Well, OK, I will be around tomorrow so if you want to stop by then, I will be here all day.

YOU: What if I drop by around 4:00?

HOMEOWNER: Sure, sure, whatever that will be fine.

YOU: Great! I will see you then! And, Bob, thanks so much for your time!

Remember, most homeowners are not going to be thrilled to give you the appointment particularly if they have been bombarded with agent calls. Stay friendly and smile! It comes through on the phone!

COLD CALLING

If you are going to cold call, I recommend using one of your promotions to gain phone numbers and lead sheets, and then you can change the cold calling script to meet your needs.

AGENT: Hi! May speak to John please?

HOMEOWNER: Sure, who is this?

AGENT: This is David White and I am calling with XYZ Real Estate.

HOMEOWNER: Yes, this is John.

AGENT: John, as I said, I am with XYZ Real Estate and I am working in your area this month and wanted to call you and see if you could answer a couple of quick questions for me?

HOMEOWNER: Sure.

AGENT: Great! John, how long have you lived in the area?

HOMEOWNER: Three years.

AGENT: How do you like the area?

HOMEOWNER: It's great.

AGENT: John, did you know with home values increasing, you could possibly sell your home and make a nice profit while upgrading to another home?

HOMEOWNER: Really, that is interesting. Drop something in the mail to me about it.

AGENT: I would love to but if you have a few extra minutes after I send over the information, I would really like to talk to you further; OK?

HOMEOWNER: Sure, OK, I will look forward to it. Bye now.

CALLING REFERRALS (BUYERS)

AGENT: Hello, my I please speak with Sarah Humphreys?

HOMEOWNER: This is Sarah Humphreys

AGENT: Hi Sarah. My name is Susan Alvis and I am with XYZ Real Estate. Your friends, Don and Taylor Cox, gave me your name and number and suggested I call you.

HOMEOWNER: Really? What on earth for?

AGENT: They told me you are interested in buying real estate in the next few months and I would like to have the honor of working with you. They have told me you are interested in lake property. Is this right?

HOMEOWNER: Yes, but I cannot buy until May because of tying up some financial business.

AGENT: I understand. I just wanted to call you and say hello and ask you for your mailing address so I can send you new information about lake properties as they come on the market. Would that be OK?

HOMEOWNER: Sure, that would be great! Here is my address:

AGENT: Got it! I will just drop some information to you from time to time and when you are ready to start home shopping, do me a favor and keep me in mind, OK?

HOMEOWNER: OK! Thanks for calling!

AGENT: You are welcome. Take care. Bye.

CALLING REFERRALS (SELLERS)

AGENT: Hello, May I please speak to Michelle Dudney?

HOMEOWNER: This is Michelle.

AGENT: Hi Michelle. This is Susan Alvis and I am with XYZ Real Estate. I am calling because Mark Taylor gave me your name and number and suggested I call you.

HOMEOWNER: Mark's a good guy. He told me you would be calling.

AGENT: Great! I wanted to call and see if I could stop by your home some time in the next week or so and offer you a free market analysis on your home?

HOMEOWNER: Why?

AGENT: Mark told me you are interested in selling your home and I want to be your real estate agent. I know your area well and would love the opportunity to show you what is going on in the area. I can provide you with a market analysis to show you how much money you should be able to get out of your home as well as what has sold in the area. It helps home owners who are thinking of selling their homes so they will know what to expect.

HOMEOWNER: Oh, OK. That would be fine. I will be working in my garden all day Friday. Just stop by anytime.

AGENT: Great! I will see you then!

Final Tips, Hints, and Reminders for the Million Dollar Agent

The following tips are quick reminders for the next million dollar agent!

How to Find Properties to List:

- Canvassing on a regular basis

- Call FSBOs

- Call expired listings and inactive listings

- Work Referrals

- Take floor time

- Conduct Open Houses

- Network within your community

How to Find Buyers:

- Take Floor Calls

- Place homes magazines and business cards in public places

- Run advertisements and use billboards as budget permits

- Cold Call

- Active monthly promotions such as the described "Coming out Party"

- Network on the Internet

- Network in your community

What Not to Do Your First Year (Or Ever) in Real Estate

- Never lie to a client to make a sale

- Never forget to uphold your fiduciary duty to your client and keep all confidences

- Do not settle for scrub agent splits, go for the best splits in the business

- Do not forget your reason why

- Never forget to thank a client for a referral

Software Programs for Top Real Estate Agents

- Top Producer

- Realtor Soft

Sales Quotes for Success

- Remember the words of the wise Jeffery Gitomer, author of *The Little Red Book of Selling*: "If you make a sale you earn a commission, if you make a friend, you can earn a fortune."

- Mary Kay Ash, founder of Mary Kay Cosmetics had a

positively uplifting message that every new salesperson should adapt into their sales presentations and if they do, success will follow. She said, "Pretend that every single person you meet has a sign around his or her neck that says 'Make me feel important' and not only will you succeed in sales, you will succeed in life."

- As a new agent, the most important thing for you to remember is this anonymous quote, "Your most important sale is to sell yourself to yourself." Once you are sold on yourself and your abilities, you are already halfway there.

- "Procrastination takes time away from action" is a motto I used when I was in real estate and it served me well. It is yours to use if you want it now!

Appendix B

Canvassing Letter for the Million Dollar Agent

The following letters are samples you can send out as your first contact letter and final point of contact while working your canvassing system. Obviously, you can change the format and include as much or as little as you would like about yourself but keep in mind, it is a tool to use to introduce yourself. Also remember to ask for the business you want later. Of course, you can just use these letters by inserting your information and running with it or use these letters as a guide to design your own.

Dear Mr. and Mrs. Thompson,

Hello! I am Susan Alvis and I work with ABC Real Estate Agency. I am writing to you today to introduce myself to you and let you know I have added your name into my database so you can start receiving free newsletters about the current market conditions in our city.

As a lifelong member of the community, I know this area well and I am particularly working to become more knowledgeable about your subdivision. This is, of course, excellent news for you as a member of the Highlands Community. I will keep you up-to-date on what is selling in the area as well as market conditions and area homes for sale. In short, when it comes to real estate news in your immediate vicinity, I am going to send you everything I know over the next 12 months.

You may be wondering how much all of this is going to cost you and believe me when I tell you, it is absolutely free. I just like your neck of the woods and so I plan to become as knowledgeable about the area as possible in hopes you will remember me if you ever plan on selling your home.

Mr. and Mrs. Thompson, I stand on the belief that hard work pays off and I am willing to work hard to learn all I can about your area because your location is a great area. As you know, many buyers look for homes in your area and, therefore, when it is time for you to consider selling your home, I hope you think of me and when you do, we will find a buyer for your property.

In the meantime, enjoy your first newsletter. It has some wonderful real estate articles for you to look over, and there is even a place for you to submit your questions to me by e-mail. Also, you will notice on my Web site an area where you can send me a referral or two and if you do, I will send you a special gift as my way of saying thank you for thinking of me.

Let me know what your thoughts are on your market conditions and put me to work for you when you need a real estate professional.

All the Best,

Susan Alvis

Final Canvassing Letter Out of Rotation

Dear Mr. and Mrs. Thompson,

Thank you for allowing me to send you information on your community through market newsletters over the last year. I hope you have found the information informative and feel you have a better understanding of current market trends in your area. If you found questions left unanswered, please feel free to call me anytime and I would love to help you by answering all of your real estate questions.

At this time, I would like to invite you to stay on my mailing list, free of charge of course, for the upcoming year. If you would like to remain on my mailing list, please fill out the response card and return it to me so we can continue to stay in touch over the next year.

It has been my pleasure to bring you some of the most up-to-date information on your area. If you ever need any assistance in real estate, my hope is you will remember me. I would love to work with you in the future to help you realize your real estate dreams.

Kindest Regards,

Susan Alvis

Canvassing Phone Call Script:
Letter for Auto-Responder

The idea of a letter for your auto-responder is for you to be able to gain leads and referrals 24 hours a day without having to be directly on the computer when the lead comes into the site. The following is a sample letter you can consider adding to the auto-responder. Keep in mind, some auto-responders have the ability to personalize the letter but you will want to check with some of the programs and ask your Web designer for advice on these options.

Dear Sally,

Thank you for stopping by my Web site. I hope you enjoyed looking around the Web site. I am Susan Alvis and I have been with ABC Realty for 10 years. A lifelong resident of Ocean Springs, I enjoy working with both buyers and sellers and really look forward to talking with you soon.

Please take a moment to drop me a line to let me know what you are looking for in a property if you are considering purchasing in the Ocean Springs area. If you have a home for sale, just submit the information you do not mind sharing and I will provide you with a CMA (comparative market analysis) within 24 hours.

My office hours are Saturday through Wednesday 7 a.m. to 7 p.m. and I will contact you on my next business day so we can get to work on your real estate needs.

Again, thank you, Sally, for dropping by the site and I look forward to talking with you soon!

Kindest Regards,

Susan Alvis

About the Author

Susan Alvis has her Tennessee Real Estate License in Retirement. She writes gaming articles, books, and literary works as a ghost writer and has upcoming works in non-fiction as well as fiction. Susan lives in Northeast Tennessee with her husband, Brent and their two children, Matthew and Amber. You can visit her on her Web site at **www.SusanAlvis.com**.

Glossary: Terms New Agents Need to Know

401(k)/403(b) An investment plan sponsored by an employer that enables individuals to set aside pre-tax income for retirement or emergency purposes. 401(k) plans are provided by private corporations. 403(b) plans are provided by non-profit organizations.

401(k)/403(b) Loan A type of financing using a loan against the money accumulated in a 401(k)/403(b) plan.

Abatement Sometimes referred to as free rent or early occupancy. A condition that could happen in addition to the primary term of the lease.

Above Building Standard Finishes and specialized designs that have been upgraded in order to accommodate a tenant's requirements.

Absorption Rate The speed and amount of time at which rentable space, in square feet, is filled.

Abstract or Title Search The process of reviewing all transactions that have been recorded publicly in order to determine whether any defects in the title exist that could interfere with a clear property ownership transfer.

Accelerated Cost Recovery System A calculation for taxes to provide more depreciation for the first few years of ownership.

Accelerated Depreciation A method of depreciation where the value of a property depreciates faster in the first few years after purchasing it.

Acceleration Clause A clause in a contract that gives the lender the right to demand immediate payment of the balance of the loan if the borrower defaults on the loan.

Acceptance The seller's written approval of a buyer's offer.

Ad Valorem A Latin phrase that translates as "according to value." Refers to a tax that is imposed on a property's value that is typically based on the local government's evaluation of the property.

Addendum An addition or update for an existing contract between parties.

Additional Principal Payment Additional money paid to the lender, apart from the scheduled loan payments, to pay more of the principal balance, shortening the length of the loan.

Adjustable-Rate Mortgage (ARM) A home loan with an interest rate that is adjusted periodically in order to reflect changes in a specific financial resource.

Adjusted Funds From Operations (AFFO) The rate of REIT performance or ability to pay dividends that is used by many analysts who have concerns about the quality of earnings as measured by Funds From Operations (FFO).

Adjustment Date The date at which the interest rate is adjusted for an adjustable-rate mortgage (ARM).

Adjustment Period The amount of time between adjustments for an interest rate in an ARM.

Administrative Fee A percentage of the value of the assets under management, or a fixed annual dollar amount charged to manage an account.

Advances The payments the servicer makes when the borrower fails to send a payment.

Adviser A broker or investment banker who represents an owner in a transaction and is paid a retainer and/or a performance fee once a financing or sales transaction has closed.

Agency Closing A type of closing in which a lender uses a title company or other firm as an agent to finish a loan.

Agency Disclosure A requirement in most states that agents who act for both buyers or sellers must disclose who they are working for in the transaction.

Aggregation Risk The risk that is associated with warehousing mortgages during the process of pooling them for future security.

Agreement of Sale A legal document the buyer and seller must approve and sign that details the price and terms in the transaction.

Alienation Clause The provision in a loan that requires

the borrower to pay the total balance of the loan at once if the property is sold or the ownership transferred.

Alternative Mortgage A home loan that does not match the standard terms of a fixed-rate mortgage.

Alternative or Specialty Investments Types of property that are not considered to be conventional real estate investments, such as self-storage facilities, mobile homes, timber, agriculture, or parking lots.

Amortization The usual process of paying a loan's interest and principal via scheduled monthly payments.

Amortization Schedule A chart or table that shows the percentage of each payment that will be applied toward principal and interest over the life of the mortgage and how the loan balance decreases until it reaches zero.

Amortization Tables The mathematical tables that are used to calculate what a borrower's monthly payment will be.

Amortization Term The number of months it will take to amortize the loan.

Anchor The business or individual who is serving as the primary draw to a commercial property.

Annual Mortgagor Statement A yearly statement to borrowers which details the remaining principal balance and amounts paid throughout the year for taxes and interest.

Annual Percentage Rate (APR) The interest rate that states the actual cost of borrowing money over the course of a year.

Annuity The regular payments of a fixed sum.

Application The form a borrower must complete in order to apply for a mortgage loan, including information such as income, savings, assets, and debts.

Application Fee A fee some lenders charge that may include charges for items such as property appraisal or a credit report unless those fees are included elsewhere.

Appraisal The estimate of the value of a property on a particular date given by a professional appraiser, usually presented in a written document.

Appraisal Fee The fee charged by a professional appraiser for his estimate of the market value of a property.

Appraisal Report The written report presented by an appraiser regarding the value of a property.

Appraised Value The dollar amount a professional appraiser assigned to the value of a property in his report.

Appraiser A certified individual who is qualified by education, training, and experience to estimate the value of real and personal property.

Appreciation An increase in the home's or property's value.

Appreciation Return The amount gained when the value of the real estate assets increases during the current quarter.

Arbitrage The act of buying securities in one market and selling them immediately in another market in order to profit from the difference in price.

ARM Index A number that is publicly published and used as the basis for interest rate adjustments on an ARM.

As-Is Condition A phrase in a purchase or lease contract in which the new tenant accepts the existing condition of the premises as well as any physical defects.

Assessed Value The value placed on a home that is determined by a tax assessor in order to calculate a tax base.

Assessment (1) Approximate value of a property. (2) Fee charged in addition to taxes in order to help pay for items such as water, sewer, street improvements, etc.

Assessor A public officer who estimates the value of a property for the purpose of taxation.

Asset Property or item of value owned by an individual or company.

Asset Management Fee A fee that is charged to investors based on the amount of money they have invested into real estate assets for the particular fund or account.

Asset Management The various tasks and areas around managing real estate assets from the initial investment until the time it is sold.

Asset Turnover The rate of total revenues for the previous 12 months divided by the average total assets.

Assets Under Management The amount of the current market value of real estate assets that a manager is responsible to manage and invest.

Assignee Name The individual or business to whom the lease, mortgage, or other contract has been re-assigned.

Assignment Transfer of rights and responsibilities from one party to another for paying a debt. Original party remains liable for the debt should the second party default.

Assignor The person who transfers the rights and interests of a property to another.

Assumable Mortgage A mortgage that is capable of being transferred to a different borrower.

Assumption The act of assuming the mortgage of the seller.

Assumption Clause A contractual provision that enables the buyer to take responsibility for the mortgage loan from the seller.

Assumption Fee A fee charged to the buyer for processing new records when they are assuming an existing loan.

Attorn To agree to recognize a new owner of a property and to pay rent to the new landlord.

Average Common Equity The sum of the common equity for the last five quarters divided by five.

Average Downtime The number of months that are expected between a lease's expiration and the beginning of a replacement lease under the current market conditions.

Average Free Rent The number of months the rent abatement concession is expected to be granted to a tenant as part of an incentive to lease under current market conditions.

Average Occupancy Average rate of each of the previous 12 months that a property was occupied.

Average Total Assets The sum of the total assets of a company for the previous five quarters divided by five.

Back Title Letter A letter an attorney receives from a title insurance company before examining the title for insurance purposes.

Back-End Ratio The calculation lenders use to compare a borrower's gross monthly income to their total debt.

Balance Sheet A statement that lists an individual's assets, liabilities, and net worth.

Balloon Loan A type of mortgage in which the monthly payments are not large enough to repay the loan by the end of the term, and the final payment is one large payment of the remaining balance.

Balloon Payment The final huge payment due at the end of a balloon mortgage.

Balloon Risk The risk that a borrower may not be able to come up with the funds for the balloon payment at maturity.

Bankrupt The state an individual or business is in if they are unable to repay their debt when it is due.

Bankruptcy Legal proceeding where a debtor can obtain relief from payment of certain obligations by restructuring their finances.

Base Loan Amount The amount that forms the basis for the loan payments.

Base Principal Balance Original loan amount once adjustments for subsequent fundings and principal payments have been made without including accrued interest or other unpaid debts.

Base Rent A certain amount that is used as a minimum rent, providing for rent increases over the term of the lease agreement.

Base Year The sum of actual taxes and operating expenses during a given year, often that in which a lease begins.

Basis Point A term for 1/100 of one percentage point.

Before-Tax Income An individual's income before taxes have been deducted.

Below-Grade Any structure or part of a structure that is below the surface of the ground that surrounds it.

Beneficiary An employee who is covered by the benefit plan his or her company provides.

Beta Measurement of common stock price volatility for a company in comparison to the market.

Bid The price or range an investor is willing to spend on whole loans or securities.

Bill of Sale A written legal document that transfers the ownership of personal property to another party.

Binder (1) A report describing the conditions of a property's title. (2) An early agreement between seller and buyer.

Biweekly Mortgage A mortgage repayment plan that requires payments every two weeks to help repay the loan over a shorter amount of time.

Blanket Mortgage A rare type of mortgage that covers more than one of the borrower's properties.

Blind Pool A mixed fund that accepts capital from investors without specifying property assets.

Bond Market The daily buying and selling of thirty-year treasury bonds that also affects fixed rate mortgages.

Book Value The value of a property based on its purchase amount plus upgrades or other additions with depreciation subtracted.

Break-Even Point The point at which a landlord's income from rent matches expenses and debt.

Bridge Loan A short-term loan for individuals or companies that are still seeking more permanent financing.

Broker A person who serves as a go-between for a buyer and seller.

Brokerage The process of bringing two or more parties together in exchange for a fee, commission, or other compensation.

Buildable Acres The portion of land that can be built on after allowances for roads, setbacks, anticipated open spaces, and unsuitable areas have been made.

Building Code The laws set forth by the local government regarding end use of a given piece of property. These law codes may dictate the design, materials used, and/or types of improvements that will be allowed.

Building Standard Plus Allowance A detailed list provided by the landlord stating the standard building materials and costs necessary to make the premises inhabitable.

Build-Out Improvements to a property's space that have been implemented according to the tenant's specifications.

Build-to-Suit A way of leasing property, usually for commercial purposes, in which the developer or landlord builds to a tenant's specifications.

Buydown A term that usually refers to a fixed-rate mortgage for which additional payments can be applied to the interest rate for a temporary period, lowering payments for a period of one to three years.

Buydown Mortgage A style of home loan in which the lender receives a higher payment in order to convince them to reduce the interest rate during the initial years of the mortgage.

Buyer's Remorse A nervousness that first-time home buyers tend to feel after signing a sales contract or closing the purchase of a house.

Call Date The periodic or continuous right a lender has to call for payment of the total remaining balance prior to the date of maturity.

Call Option A clause in a loan agreement that allows a lender to demand repayment of the entire principal balance at any time.

Cap A limit on how much the monthly payment or interest rate is allowed to increase in an adjustable-rate mortgage.

Capital Appreciation The change in a property's or portfolio's market value after it has been adjusted for capital improvements and partial sales.

Capital Expenditures The purchase of long-term assets, or the expansion of existing ones, that prolongs the life or efficiency of those assets.

Capital Gain The amount of excess when the net proceeds from the sale of an asset are higher than its book value.

Capital Improvements Expenses that prolong the life of a property or add new improvements to it.

Capital Markets Public and private markets where individuals or businesses can raise or borrow capital.

Capitalization The mathematical process that investors use to derive the value of a property using the rate of return on investments.

Capitalization Rate Percentage of return as it is estimated from the net income of a property.

Carryback Financing A type of funding in which a seller agrees to hold back a note for a specified portion of the sales price.

Carrying Charges Costs incurred to the landlord when initially leasing out a property and then during the periods of vacancy.

Cash Flow The amount of income an investor receives on a rental property after operating expenses and loan payments have been deducted.

Cashier's Check A check the bank draws on its own resources instead of a depositor's account.

Cash-on-Cash Yield The

percentage of a property's net cash flow and the average amount of invested capital during the specified operating year.

Cash-Out Refinance The act of refinancing a mortgage for an amount that is higher than the original amount for the purpose of using the leftover cash for personal use.

Certificate of Deposit A type of deposit that is held in a bank for a limited time and pays a certain amount of interest to the depositor.

Certificate of Deposit Index (CODI) A rate that is based on interest rates of six-month CDs and is often used to determine interest rates for some ARMs.

Certificate of Eligibility A type of document that the Department of Veterans Affairs issues to verify the eligibility of a veteran for a VA loan.

Certificate of Occupancy (CO) A written document issued by a local government or building agency that states that a home or other building is inhabitable after meeting all building codes.

Certificate of Reasonable Value (CRV) An appraisal presented by the Department of Veterans Affairs that shows the current market value of a property.

Certificate of Veteran Status A document veterans or reservists receive if they have served 90 days of continuous active duty (including training time).

Chain of Title The official record of all transfers of ownership over the history of a piece of property.

Chapter 11 The part of the federal bankruptcy code that deals with reorganizations of businesses.

Chapter 7 The part of the federal bankruptcy code that deals with liquidations of businesses.

Circulation Factor The interior space that is required for internal office circulation and is not included in the net square footage.

Class A A property rating that is usually assigned to those that will generate the maximum rent per square foot, due to superior quality and/or location.

Class B A good property most potential tenants would find desirable but lacks certain attributes that would bring in the top dollar.

Class C A building that is physically acceptable but offers few amenities, thereby becoming cost-effective space for tenants who are seeking a particular image.

Clear Title A property title that is free of liens, defects, or other legal encumbrances.

Clear-Span Facility A type of building, usually a warehouse or parking garage, consisting of vertical columns on the outer edges of the structure and clear spaces between the columns.

Closed-End Fund A mixed fund with a planned range of investor capital and a limited life.

Closing The final act of procuring a loan and title in which documents are signed between the buyer and seller and/or their respective representation and all money concerned in the contract changes hands.

Closing Costs The expenses that are related to the sale of real estate including loan, title, and appraisal fees and are beyond the price of the property itself.

Closing Statement See: Settlement Statement.

Cloud on Title Certain conditions uncovered in a title search that present a negative impact to the title for the property.

Commercial Mortgage-Backed Securities (CMBS) A type of securities that is backed by loans on commercial real estate.

Collateralized Mortgage Obligation (CMO) Debt that is fully based on a pool of mortgages.

Co-Borrower Another individual who is jointly responsible for the loan and is on the title to the property.

Cost of Funds Index (COFI) An index used to determine changes in the interest rates for certain ARMs.

Co-Investment Program A separate account for an insurance company or investment partnership in which two or more pension funds may co-invest their capital in an individual property or a portfolio of properties.

Co-Investment The condition that occurs when two or more pension funds or groups of funds are sharing ownership of a real estate investment.

Collateral The property for which a borrower has obtained a loan, thereby assuming the risk of losing the property if the loan is not repaid according to the terms of the loan agreement.

Collection The effort on the part of a lender, due to a borrower defaulting on a loan, which involves mailing and recording certain documents in the event that the foreclosure procedure must be implemented.

Commercial Mortgage A loan used to purchase a piece of commercial property or building.

Commercial Mortgage Broker A broker specialized in commercial mortgage applications.

Commercial Mortgage Lender A lender specialized in funding commercial mortgage loans.

Commingled Fund A pooled fund that enables qualified employee benefit plans to mix their capital in order to achieve professional management, greater diversification, or investment positions in larger properties.

Commission A compensation to salespeople that is paid out of the total amount of the purchase transaction.

Commitment The agreement of a lender to make a loan with given terms for a specific period.

Commitment Fee The fee a lender charges for the guarantee of specified loan terms, to be honored at some point in the future.

Common Area Assessments Sometimes called Homeowners' Association Fees. Charges paid to the homeowners' association by the individual unit owners, in a condominium or planned unit development (PUD), that are usually used to maintain the property and common areas.

Common Area Maintenance The additional charges the tenant must pay in addition to the base rent to pay for the maintenance of common areas.

Common Areas The portions of a building, land, and amenities, owned or managed by a planned unit development or condominium's homeowners' association, that are used by all of the unit owners who share in the common expense of operation and maintenance.

Common Law A set of unofficial laws that were originally based on English customs and used to some extent in several states.

Community Property Property that is acquired by a married couple during the course of their marriage and is considered in many states to be owned jointly, unless certain circumstances are in play.

Comparable Sales Also called Comps or Comparables. The recent selling prices of similar properties in the area that are used to help determine the market value of a property.

Compound Interest The amount of interest paid on the principal balance of a mortgage in addition to accrued interest.

Concessions Cash, or the equivalent, that the landlord pays or allows in the form of rental abatement, additional tenant finish allowance, moving expenses, or other costs expended in order to persuade a tenant to sign a lease.

Condemnation A government agency's act of taking private property, without the owner's consent, for public use through the power of eminent domain.

Conditional Commitment A

lender's agreement to make a loan providing the borrower meets certain conditions.

Conditional Sale A contract to sell a property that states that the seller will retain the title until all contractual conditions have been fulfilled.

Condominium A type of ownership in which all of the unit owners own the property, common areas, and buildings jointly, and have sole ownership in the unit to which they hold the title.

Condominium Conversion Changing an existing rental property's ownership to the condominium form of ownership.

Condominium Hotel A condominium project that involves registration desks, short-term occupancy, food and telephone services, and daily cleaning services, and is generally operated as a commercial hotel even though the units are individually owned.

Conduit A strategic alliance between lenders and unaffiliated organizations that acts as a source of funding by regularly purchasing loans, usually with a goal of pooling and securitizing them.

Conforming Loan A type of mortgage that meets the conditions to be purchased by Fannie Mae or Freddie Mac.

Construction Documents The drawings and specifications an architect and/or engineer provides to describe construction requirements for a project.

Construction Loan Short-term loan to finance the cost of construction, usually dispensed in stages throughout the construction project.

Construction Management The process of ensuring that the stages of the construction project are completed in a timely and seamless manner.

Construction-to-Permanent Loan A construction loan that can be converted to a longer-term traditional mortgage after construction is complete.

Consultant Any individual or company that provides the services to institutional investors, such as defining real estate investment policies, making recommendations to advisers or managers, analyzing existing real estate portfolios, monitoring and reporting on portfolio performance, and/or reviewing specified investment opportunities.

Consumer Price Index (CPI) A measurement of inflation, relating to the change in the prices of goods and services that are regularly purchased by a specific population during a certain period of time.

Contiguous Space Refers to several suites or spaces on a floor (or connected floors) in a given building that can be combined and rented to a single tenant.

Contingency Specific condition that must be met before either party in a contract can be legally bound.

Contract An agreement, either verbal or written, to perform or not to perform a certain thing.

Contract Documents See: Construction Documents.

Contract Rent Also known as Face Rent. The dollar amount of the rental obligation specified in a lease.

Conventional Loan A long-term loan from a non-governmental lender that a borrower obtains for the purchase of a home.

Convertible Adjustable-Rate Mortgage Type of mortgage that begins as a traditional ARM but contains a provision to enable the borrower to change to a fixed-rate mortgage during a certain period of time.

Convertible Debt The point in a mortgage at which the lender has the option to convert to a partially or fully owned property within a certain period of time.

Convertible Preferred Stock Preferred stock that can be

converted to common stock under certain conditions that have been specified by the issuer.

Conveyance The act of transferring a property title between parties by deed.

Cooperative Also called a Co-op. A type of ownership by multiple residents of a multi-unit housing complex in which they all own shares in the cooperative corporation that owns the property, thereby having the right to occupy a particular apartment or unit.

Cooperative Mortgage Any loan that is related to a cooperative residential project.

Core Properties The main types of property, specifically office, retail, industrial, and multi-family.

Co-Signer A second individual or party who also signs a promissory note or loan agreement, thereby taking responsibility for the debt in the event that the primary borrower cannot pay.

Cost-Approach Improvement Value The current expenses for constructing a copy or replacement for an existing structure, but subtracting an estimate of the accrued depreciation.

Cost-Approach Land Value The estimated value of the basic interest in the land, as if it were available for development to its highest and best use.

Cost-of-Sale Percentage An estimate of the expenses of selling an investment that represents brokerage commissions, closing costs, fees, and other necessary sales costs.

Coupon The token or expected interest rate the borrower is charged on a promissory note or mortgage.

Courier Fee The fee that is charged at closing for the delivery of documents between all parties concerned in a real estate transaction.

Covenant A written agreement, included in deeds or other legal documents, that defines the requirements for certain acts or use of a property.

Credit An agreement in which a borrower promises to repay the lender at a later date and receives something of value in exchange.

Credit Enhancement The necessary credit support, in addition to mortgage collateral, in order to achieve the desired credit rating on mortgage-backed securities.

Credit History An individual's record which details his current and past financial obligations and performance.

Credit Life Insurance A type of insurance that pays the balance of a mortgage if the borrower dies.

Credit Rating Degree of creditworthiness a person is assigned based on credit history and current financial status.

Credit Report A record detailing an individual's credit, employment, and residence history used to determine the individual's creditworthiness.

Credit Repository A company that records and updates credit applicants' financial and credit information from various sources.

Credit Score Sometimes called a Credit Risk Score. The number contained in a consumer's credit report that represents a statistical summary of the information.

Creditor A party to whom other parties owe money.

Cross-Collateralization A group of mortgages or properties that jointly secures one debt obligation.

Cross-Defaulting A provision that allows a trustee or lender to require full payment on all loans in a group, if any single loan in the group is in default.

Cumulative Discount Rate A percentage of the current value of base rent with all landlord lease concessions taken into account.

Current Occupancy The current percentage of units in a building or property that is leased.

Current Yield The annual rate of return on an investment, expressed as a percentage.

Deal Structure The type of agreement in financing an acquisition. The deal can be un-leveraged, leveraged, traditional debt, participating debt, participating/convertible debt, or joint ventures.

Debt Any amount one party owes to another party.

Debt Service Coverage Ratio (DSCR) A property's yearly net operating income divided by the yearly cost of debt service.

Debt Service The amount of money that is necessary to meet all interest and principal payments during a specific period.

Debt-to-Income Ratio The percentage of a borrower's monthly payment on long-term debts divided by his gross monthly income.

Dedicate To change a private property to public ownership for a particular public use.

Deed A legal document that conveys property ownership to the buyer.

Deed in Lieu of Foreclosure A situation in which a deed is given to a lender in order to satisfy a mortgage debt and to avoid the foreclosure process.

Deed of Trust A provision that allows a lender to foreclose on a property in the event that the borrower defaults on the loan.

Default The state that occurs when a borrow fails to fulfill a duty or take care of an obligation, such as making monthly mortgage payments.

Deferred Maintenance Account A type of account that a borrower must fund to provide for maintenance of a property.

Deficiency Judgment The legal assignment of personal liability to a borrower for the unpaid balance of a mortgage, after foreclosing on the property has failed to yield the full amount of the debt.

Defined-Benefit Plan A type of benefit provided by an employer that defines an employee's benefits either as a fixed amount or a percentage of the beneficiary's salary when he retires.

Defined-Contribution Plan A type of benefit plan provided by an employer in which an employee's retirement benefits are determined by the amount that has been contributed by the employer and/or employee during the time of employment, and by the actual investment earnings on those contributions over the life of the fund.

Delinquency A state that occurs when the borrower fails to make mortgage payments on time, eventually resulting in foreclosure, if severe enough.

Delinquent Mortgage A mortgage in which the borrower is behind on payments.

Demising Wall The physical partition between the spaces of two tenants or from the building's common areas.

Deposit Also referred to as Earnest Money. The funds that the buyer provides when offering to purchase property.

Depreciation A decline in the value of property or an asset, often used as a tax-deductible item.

Derivative Securities A type of securities that has been created from other financial instruments.

Design/Build An approach in which a single individual or business is responsible for both the design and construction.

Disclosure A written statement, presented to a potential buyer, that lists information relevant to a piece of property, whether positive or negative.

Discount Points Fees that a lender charges in order to provide a lower interest rate.

Discount Rate A figure used to translate present value from future payments or receipts.

Discretion The amount of authority an adviser or manager is granted for investing and managing a client's capital.

Distraint The act of seizing a tenant's personal property when the tenant is in default, based on the right the landlord has in satisfying the debt.

Diversification Act of spreading individual investments out to insulate a portfolio against the risk of reduced yield or capital loss.

Dividend Yield Percentage of a security's market price that represents the annual dividend rate.

Dividend Distributions of cash or stock that stockholders receive.

Dividend-Ex Date Initial date on which a person purchasing the stock can no longer receive the most recently announced dividend.

Document Needs List The list of documents a lender requires from a potential borrower who is submitting a loan application.

Documentation Preparation Fee A fee that lenders, brokers, and/ or settlement agents charge for the preparation of the necessary closing documents.

Dollar Stop Agreed amount of taxes and operating expenses each tenant must pay out on a prorated basis.

Down Payment The variance between the purchase price and the portion that the mortgage lender financed.

DOWNREIT A structure of organization that makes it possible for REITs to purchase properties using partnership units.

Draw A payment from the construction loan proceeds made to contractors, subcontractors, home builders, or suppliers.

Due Diligence The activities of a prospective purchaser or mortgager of real property for the purpose of confirming that the property is as represented by the seller and is not subject to environmental or other problems.

Due on Sale Clause The standard mortgage language that states the loan must still be repaid if the property is resold.

Earnest Money See: Deposit.

Earthquake Insurance A type of insurance policy that provides coverage against earthquake damage to a home.

Easement Right given to a non-ownership party to use a certain part of the property for specified purposes, such as servicing power lines or cable lines.

Economic Feasibility The viability of a building or project in terms of costs and revenue where the degree of viability is established by extra revenue.

Economic Rent The market rental value of a property at a particular point in time.

Effective Age An estimate of the physical condition of a building presented by an appraiser.

Effective Date The date on which the sale of securities can commence once a registration statement becomes effective.

Effective Gross Income (EGI) The total property income that rents and other sources generate after subtracting a vacancy factor estimated to be appropriate for the property.

Effective Gross Rent (EGR) The net rent generated after adjusting for tenant improvements and other capital costs, lease commissions, and other sales expenses.

Effective Rent Actual rental rate the landlord achieves after deducting the concession value from the base rental rate a tenant pays.

Electronic Authentication A way of providing proof that a particular electronic document is genuine, has arrived unaltered, and came from the indicated source.

Eminent Domain Power of the government to pay the fair market value for a property, appropriating it for public use.

Encroachment Any improvement or upgrade that illegally intrudes onto another party's property.

Encumbrance Any right or interest in a property that interferes with using it or transferring ownership.

End Loan The result of converting to permanent financing from a construction loan.

Entitlement A benefit of a VA home loan. Often referred to as Eligibility.

Environmental Impact Statement Legally required documents that must accompany major project proposals where there will likely be an impact on the surrounding environment.

Equal Credit Opportunity Act (ECOA) Federal law that requires a lender or other creditor to make credit available for applicants regardless of sex, marital status, race, religion, or age.

Equifax One of the three primary credit-reporting bureaus.

Equity The value of a property after existing liabilities have been deducted.

Employee Retirement Income Security Act (ERISA) A legislation that controls the investment activities, mainly of corporate and union pension plans.

Errors and Omissions Insurance
A type of policy that insures against the mistakes of a builder or architect.

Escalation Clause The clause in a lease that provides for the rent to be increased to account for increases in the expenses the landlord must pay.

Escrow A valuable item, money, or documents deposited with a third party for delivery upon the fulfillment of a condition.

Escrow Account Also referred to as an Impound Account. An account established by a mortgage lender or servicing company for the purpose of holding funds for the payment of items, such as homeowner's insurance and property taxes.

Escrow Agent A neutral third party who makes sure that all conditions of a real estate transaction have been met before any funds are transferred or property is recorded.

Escrow Agreement Written agreement between an escrow agent and the contractual parties that defines the basic obligations of each party, the money (or other valuables) to be deposited in escrow, and how the escrow agent is to dispose of the money on deposit.

Escrow Analysis An annual investigation a lender performs to make sure they are collecting the appropriate amount of money for anticipated expenditures.

Escrow Closing The event in which all conditions of a real estate transaction have been met, and the property title is transferred to the buyer.

Escrow Company A neutral company that serves as a third party to ensure that all conditions of a real estate transaction are met.

Escrow Disbursements The dispensing of escrow funds for the payment of real estate taxes, hazard insurance, mortgage insurance, and other property expenses as they are due.

Escrow Payment The funds that are withdrawn by a mortgage servicer from a borrower's escrow account to pay property taxes and insurance.

Estate Total assets, including property, of an individual after he has died.

Estimated Closing Costs An estimation of the expenses relating to the sale of real estate.

Estimated Hazard Insurance An estimation of hazard insurance, or homeowner's insurance, that will cover physical risks.

Estimated Property Taxes An estimation of the property taxes that must be paid on the property, according to state and county tax rates.

Estoppel Certificate A signed statement that certifies that certain factual statements are correct as of the date of the statement and can be relied upon by a third party, such as a prospective lender or purchaser.

Eviction The legal removal of an occupant from a piece of property.

Examination of Title A title company's inspection and report of public records and other documents for the purpose of determining the chain of ownership of a property.

Exclusive Agency Listing A written agreement between a property owner and a real estate broker in which the owner promises to pay the broker a commission if certain property is leased during the listing period.

Exclusive Listing A contract that allows a licensed real estate agent to be the only agent who can sell a property for a given time.

Executed Contract An agreement in which all parties involved have fulfilled their duties.

Executor The individual who is named in a will to administer an estate. Executrix is the feminine form.

Exit Strategy An approach investors may use when they wish to liquidate all or part of their investment.

Experian One of the three primary credit-reporting bureaus.

Face Rental Rate The rental rate that the landlord publishes.

Facility Space The floor area in a hospitality property that is dedicated to activities, such as restaurants, health clubs, and gift shops, that interactively service multiple people and is not directly related to room occupancy.

Funds Available for Distribution (FAD) The income from operations, with cash expenditures subtracted, that may be used for leasing commissions and tenant improvement costs.

FAD Multiple The price per share of a REIT divided by its funds available for distribution.

Fair Credit Reporting Act (FCRA) The federal legislation that governs the processes credit reporting agencies must follow.

Fair Housing Act The federal legislation that prohibits the refusal to rent or sell to anyone based on race, color, religion, sex, family status, or disability.

Fair Market Value The highest price that a buyer would be willing to pay, and the lowest a seller would be willing to accept.

Fannie Mae See: Federal National Mortgage Association.

Fannie Mae's Community Home Buyer's Program A community lending model based on borrower income in which mortgage insurers and Fannie Mae offer flexible underwriting guidelines in order to increase the buying power for a low- or moderate-income family and to decrease the total amount of cash needed to purchase a home.

Farmer's Home Administration (FMHA) An agency within the U.S. Department of Agriculture that provides credit to farmers and other rural residents.

Federal Home Loan Mortgage Corporation (FHLMC) Also known as Freddie Mac. The company that buys mortgages from lending institutions, combines them with other loans, and sells shares to investors.

Federal Housing Administration (FHA) A government agency that provides low-rate mortgages to buyers who are able to make a down payment as low as 3 percent.

Federal National Mortgage Association (FNMA) Also known as Fannie Mae. A congressionally chartered, shareholder-owned company that is the nation's largest supplier of home mortgage funds. The company buys mortgages from lenders and resells them as securities on the secondary mortgage market.

Fee Simple The highest possible interest a person can have in a piece of real estate.

Fee Simple Estate An unconditional, unlimited inheritance estate in which the owner may dispose of or use the property as desired.

Fee Simple Interest The state of owning all the rights in a real estate parcel.

Funds From Operations (FFO) A ratio that is meant to highlight the amount of cash a company's real estate portfolio generates relative to its total operating cash flow.

FFO Multiple The price of a REIT share divided by its funds from operations.

FHA Loans Mortgages that the Federal Housing Administration (FHA) insures.

FHA Mortgage Insurance A type of insurance that requires a fee to be paid at closing in order to insure the loan with the Federal Housing Administration (FHA).

Fiduciary Any individual who holds authority over a plan's asset management, administration or disposition, or renders paid investment advice regarding a plan's assets.

Finance Charge The amount of interest to be paid on a loan or credit card balance.

Firm Commitment A written agreement a lender makes to loan money for the purchase of property.

First Mortgage The main mortgage on a property.

First Refusal Right/ Right of First Refusal Lease clause that gives a tenant the first opportunity to buy a property or to lease additional space in a property at the same price and terms as those contained in an offer from a third party that the owner has expressed a willingness to accept.

First-Generation Space A new space that has never before been occupied by a tenant and is currently available for lease.

First-Loss Position A security's position that will suffer the first economic loss if the assets below it lose value or are foreclosed on.

Fixed Costs Expenses that remain the same despite the level of sales or production.

Fixed Rate Interest rate that does not change over the life of the loan.

Fixed Time The particular weeks of a year that the owner of a timeshare arrangement can access his or her accommodations.

Fixed-Rate Mortgage A loan with an unchanging interest rate over the life of the loan.

Fixture Items that become a part of the property when they are permanently attached to the property.

Flat Fee An amount of money that an adviser or manager receives for managing a portfolio of real estate assets.

Flex Space A building that provides a flexible configuration of office or showroom space combined with manufacturing, laboratory, warehouse, distribution, etc.

Float The number of freely traded shares owned by the public.

Flood Certification The process of analyzing whether a property is located in a known flood zone.

Flood Insurance A policy that is required in designated flood zones to protect against loss due to flood damage.

Floor Area Ratio (FAR) A measurement of a building's gross square footage compared to the square footage of the land on which it is located.

For Sale By Owner (FSBO) A method of selling property in which the property owner serves as the selling agent and directly handles the sales process with the buyer or buyer's agent.

Force Majeure An external force that is not controlled by the contractual parties and prevents them from complying with the provisions of the contract.

Foreclosure The legal process in which a lender takes over ownership of a property once the borrower is in default in a mortgage arrangement.

Forward Commitments Contractual agreements to perform certain financing duties according to any stated conditions.

Four Quadrants of the Real Estate Capital Markets The four market types that consist of Private Equity, Public Equity, Private Debt, and Public Debt.

Freddie Mac See: Federal Home Loan Mortgage Corporation.

Front-End Ratio Measurement a lender uses to compare a borrower's monthly housing expense to gross monthly income.

Full Recourse A loan on which the responsibility of a loan is transferred to an endorser or guarantor in the event of default by the borrower.

Full-Service Rent A rental rate that includes all operating expenses and real estate taxes for the first year.

Fully Amortized ARM An ARM with a monthly payment that is sufficient to amortize the remaining balance at the current interest accrual rate over the amortization term.

Fully Diluted Shares The number of outstanding common stock shares if all convertible securities were converted to common shares.

Future Proposed Space The space in a commercial development that has been proposed but is not yet under construction, or the future phases of a multi-phase project that has not yet been built.

General Contractor The main person or business that contracts for the construction of an entire building or project, rather than individual duties.

General Partner The member in a partnership who holds the authority to bind the partnership and shares in its profits and losses.

Gift Money a buyer has received from a relative or other source that will not have to be repaid.

Ginnie Mae See: Government National Mortgage Association.

Going-In Capitalization Rate The rate that is computed by dividing the expected net operating income for the first year by the value of the property.

Good Faith Estimate A lender's or broker's estimate that shows all costs associated with obtaining a home loan including loan processing, title, and inspection fees.

Government Loan A mortgage that is insured or guaranteed by the FHA, the Department of Veterans Affairs (VA), or the Rural Housing Service (RHS).

Government National Mortgage Association (GNMA) Also known as Ginnie Mae. Government-owned corporation under the U.S. Department of Housing and Urban Development (HUD) that performs the same role as Fannie Mae and Freddie Mac in providing funds to lenders for making home loans, but only purchases loans backed by the federal government.

Grace Period A defined time period in which a borrower may make a loan payment after its due date without incurring a penalty.

Graduated Lease A lease, usually long-term, in which rent payments vary in accordance with future contingencies.

Graduated Payment Mortgage A mortgage that requires low payments during the first years of the loan, but eventually requires larger monthly payments over the term of the loan that become fixed later in the term.

Grant To give or transfer an interest in a property by deed or other documented method.

Grantee The party to whom an interest in a property is given.

Grantor Party who is transferring an interest in a property.

Gross Building Area Sum of areas at all floor levels, including the basement, mezzanine, and penthouses included in the principal outside faces of the exterior walls without allowing for architectural setbacks or projections.

Gross Income The total income of a household before taxes or expenses have been subtracted.

Gross Investment in Real Estate (Historic Cost) The total amount of equity and debt that is invested in a piece of real estate minus proceeds from sales or partial sales.

Gross Leasable Area Amount of floor space designed for tenants' occupancy and exclusive use.

Gross Lease A rental arrangement in which the tenant pays a flat sum for rent, and the landlord must pay all building expenses out of that amount.

Gross Real Estate Asset Value Total market value of the real estate investments under management in a fund or individual accounts, usually including the total value of all equity positions, debt positions, and joint venture ownership positions.

Gross Real Estate Investment Value The market value of real estate investments that are held in a portfolio without including debt.

Gross Returns The investment returns generated from operating a property without adjusting for adviser or manager fees.

Ground Lease Land being leased to an individual that has absolutely no residential dwelling on the property; or if it does, the ground (or land) is the only portion of the property being leased.

Ground Rent A long-term lease in which rent is paid to the land owner, normally to build something on that land.

Growing-Equity Mortgage Fixed-rate mortgage in which payments increase over a specified amount of time with the extra funds being applied to the principal.

Guarantor Party who makes a guaranty.

Guaranty Agreement in which the guarantor promises to satisfy the debt or obligations of another, if and when the debtor fails to do so.

Hard Cost The expenses attributed to actually constructing property improvements.

Hazard Insurance Also known as **Homeowner's Insurance or Fire Insurance.** A policy that provides coverage for damage from forces such as fire and wind.

Highest and Best Use The most reasonable, expected, legal use of a piece of vacant land or improved property that is physically possible, supported appropriately, financially feasible, and that results in the highest value.

High-Rise In a suburban district, any building taller than six stories. In a business district, any building taller than 25 stories.

Holdbacks A portion of a loan funding that is not dispersed until an additional condition is met, such as the completion of construction.

Holding Period Expected length of time, from purchase to sale, that an investor will own a property.

Hold-Over Tenant A tenant who retains possession of the leased premises after the lease has expired.

Home Equity Conversion Mortgage (HECM) Also referred to as a Reverse Annuity Mortgage. Type of mortgage in which the lender makes payments to the owner, thereby enabling older homeowners to convert equity in their homes into cash in the form of monthly payments.

Home Equity Line Open-ended amount of credit based on equity a homeowner has accumulated.

Home Equity Loan A type of loan that allows owners to borrow against the equity in their homes up to a limited amount.

Home Inspection A pre-purchase examination of the condition a home is in by a certified inspector.

Home Inspector A certified professional who determines the structural soundness and operating systems of a property.

Home Price The price that a buyer and seller agree upon, generally based on the home's appraised market value.

Homeowners' Association (HOA) Group that governs a community, condominium building, or neighborhood and enforces the covenants, conditions, and restrictions set by the developer.

Homeowners' Association Dues The monthly payments that are paid to the homeowners' association for maintenance and communal expenses.

Homeowner's Insurance A policy that includes coverage for all damages that may affect the value of a house as defined in the terms of the insurance policy.

Homeowner's Warranty Type of policy home buyers often purchase to cover repairs, such as heating or air-conditioning, should they stop working within the coverage period.

Homestead The property an owner uses as his primary residence.

Housing Expense Ratio The percentage of gross income that is devoted to housing costs each month.

HUD (Housing and Urban Development) A federal agency that oversees a variety of housing and community development programs, including the FHA.

HUD Median Income Average income for families in a particular area, which is estimated by HUD.

HUD-1 Settlement Statement Also known as the Closing Statement or Settlement Sheet. Itemized listing of the funds paid at closing.

HUD-1 Uniform Settlement Statement A closing statement for the buyer and seller that describes all closing costs for a real estate transaction or refinancing.

HVAC Heating, ventilating, and air-conditioning.

Hybrid Debt A position in a mortgage that has equity-like features of participation in both cash flow and the appreciation of the property at the point of sale or refinance.

Implied Cap Rate Net operating income divided by the sum of a REIT's equity market capitalization and its total outstanding debt.

Impounds Part of the monthly mortgage payment that is reserved in an account in order to pay for hazard insurance, property taxes, and private mortgage insurance.

Improvements The upgrades or changes made to a building to improve its value or usefulness.

Incentive Fee A structure in which the fee amount charged is based on the performance of the real estate assets under management.

Income Capitalization Value The figure derived for an income-producing property by converting its expected benefits into property value.

Income Property A particular property used to generate income but not occupied by the owner.

Income Return The percentage of the total return generated by the income from property, fund, or account operations.

Index A financial table that lenders use for calculating interest rates on ARMs.

Indexed Rate Sum of the published index with a margin added.

Indirect Costs Expenses of development other than the costs of direct material and labor that are related directly to the construction of improvements.

Individual Account Management Process of maintaining accounts that have been established for individual plan sponsors or other investors for investment in real estate, where a firm acts as an adviser in obtaining and/or managing a real estate portfolio.

Inflation Hedge Investment whose value tends to increase at a greater rate than inflation, contributing to the preservation of the purchasing power of a portfolio.

Inflation Rate at which consumer prices increase each year.

Initial Interest Rate The original interest rate on an ARM which is sometimes subject to a variety of adjustments throughout the mortgage.

Initial Public Offering (IPO) The first time a previously private company offers securities for public sale.

Initial Rate Cap The limit specified by some ARMs as the maximum amount the interest rate may increase when the initial interest rate expires.

Initial Rate Duration The date specified by most ARMs at which the initial rate expires.

Inspectio0n Fee The fee a licensed property inspector charges for determining the current physical condition of the property.

Inspection Report A written report of the property's condition presented by a licensed inspection professional.

Institutional-Grade Property A variety of types of real estate properties usually owned or financed by tax-exempt institutional investors.

Insurance Binder Temporary insurance policy that is implemented while a permanent policy is drawn up or obtained.

Insurance Company Separate Account Real estate investment vehicle only offered by life insurance companies, which enables an ERISA-governed fund to avoid creating unrelated taxable income for certain types of property investments and investment structures.

Insured Mortgage Mortgage that is guaranteed by the FHA or by private mortgage insurance (PMI).

Interest Accrual Rate The rate at which a mortgage accrues interest.

Interest-Only Loan A mortgage for which the borrower pays only the interest that accrues on the loan balance each month.

Interest Paid over Life of Loan The total amount that has been paid to the lender during the time the money was borrowed.

Interest Rate Percentage charged for a loan.

Interest Rate Buy-Down Plans A plan in which a seller uses funds from the sale of the home to buy down the interest rate and reduce the buyer's monthly payments.

Interest Rate Cap The highest interest rate charge allowed on the monthly payment of an ARM during an adjustment period.

Interest Rate Ceiling The maximum interest rate a lender can charge for an ARM.

Interest Rate Floor The minimum possible interest rate a lender can charge for an ARM.

Interest The price that is paid for the use of capital.

Interest-Only Strip A derivative security that consists of all or part of the portion of interest in the underlying loan or security.

Interim Financing Also known as Bridge or Swing Loans. Short-term financing a seller uses to bridge the gap between the sale of one house and the purchase of another.

Internal Rate of Return (IRR) The calculation of a discounted cash flow analysis that is used to determine the potential total return of a real estate asset during a particular holding period.

Inventory The entire space of a certain proscribed market without concern for its availability or condition.

Investment Committee Governing body charged with overseeing corporate pension investments and developing investment policies for board approval.

Investment Manager An individual or company that assumes authority over a specified amount of real estate capital, invests that capital in assets using a separate account, and provides asset management.

Investment Policy A document that formalizes an institution's goals, objectives, and guidelines for asset management, investment advisory contracting, fees, and utilization of consultants and other outside professionals.

Investment Property Piece of real estate that generates some form of income.

Investment Strategy Methods used by a manager in structuring a portfolio and selecting the real estate assets for a fund or an account.

Investment Structures Approaches to investing that include un-leveraged acquisitions, leveraged acquisitions, traditional debt, participating debt, convertible debt, triple-net leases, and joint ventures.

Investment-Grade CMBS Commercial mortgage-backed securities that have ratings of AAA, AA, A, or BBB.

Investor Status The position an investor is in, either taxable or tax-exempt.

Joint Liability The condition in which responsibility rests with two or more people for fulfilling the terms of a home loan or other financial debt.

Joint Tenancy Form of ownership in which two or more people have equal shares in a piece of property, and rights pass to the surviving owner(s) in the event of death.

Joint Venture An investment business formed by more than one party for the purpose of acquiring or developing and managing property and/or other assets.

Judgment Decision a court of law makes.

Judicial Foreclosure The usual foreclosure proceeding some states use, which is handled in a civil lawsuit.

Jumbo Loan Type of mortgage that exceeds the required limits set by Fannie Mae and Freddie Mac each year.

Junior Mortgage Loan that is a lower priority behind the primary loan.

Just Compensation The amount that is fair to both the owner and the government when property is appropriated for public use through eminent domain.

Landlord's Warrant The warrant a landlord obtains to take a tenant's personal property to sell at a public sale to compel payment of the rent or other stipulation in the lease.

Late Charge The fee that is imposed by a lender when the borrower has not made a payment when it was due.

Late Payment The payment made to the lender after the due date has passed.

Lead Manager The investment banking firm that has primary responsibility for coordinating the new issuance of securities.

Lease Contract between a property owner and tenant that defines payments and conditions under which the tenant may occupy the real estate for a given period of time.

Lease Commencement Date The date at which the terms of the lease are implemented.

Lease Expiration Exposure Schedule A chart of the total square footage of all current leases that expire in each of the next five years, without taking renewal options into account.

Lease Option A financing option that provides for home buyers to lease a home with an option to buy, with part of the rental payments being applied toward the down payment.

Leasehold Limited right to inhabit a piece of real estate held by a tenant.

Leasehold State Way of holding a property title in which the mortgagor does not actually own the property but has a long-term lease on it.

Leasehold Interest The right to hold or use property for a specific period of time at a given price without transferring ownership.

Lease-Purchase A contract that defines the closing date and solutions for the seller in the event that the buyer defaults.

Legal Blemish A negative count against a piece of property such as a zoning violation or fraudulent title claim.

Legal Description Way of describing and locating a piece of real estate recognized by law.

Legal Owner The party who holds the title to the property, although the title may carry no actual rights to the property other than as a lien.

Lender A bank or other financial institution that offers home loans.

Letter of Credit A promise from a bank or other party that the issuer will honor drafts or other requests for payment upon complying with the requirements specified in the letter of credit.

Letter of Intent　An initial agreement defining the proposed terms for the end contract.

Leverage　The process of increasing the return on an investment by borrowing some of the funds at an interest rate less than the return on the project.

Liabilities　A borrower's debts and financial obligations, whether long- or short-term.

Liability Insurance　A type of policy that protects owners against negligence, personal injury, or property damage claims.

London InterBank Offered Rate (LIBOR)　The interest rate offered on Eurodollar deposits traded between banks and used to determine changes in interest rate for ARMs.

Lien　A claim put by one party on the property of another as collateral for money owed.

Lien Waiver　A waiver of a mechanic's lien rights that is sometimes required before the general contractor can receive money under the payment provisions of a construction loan and contract.

Life Cap　A limit on the amount an ARM's interest rate can increase during the mortgage term.

Lifecycle　The stages of development for a property: pre-development, development, leasing, operating, and rehabilitation.

Lifetime Payment Cap　A limit on the amount that payments can increase or decrease over the life of an ARM.

Lifetime Rate Cap　The highest possible interest rate that may be charged, under any circumstances, over the entire life of an ARM.

Like-Kind Property　A term that refers to real estate that is held for productive use in a trade or business or for investment.

Limited Partnership　A type of partnership in which some partners manage the business and are personally liable for partnership debts, but some partners contribute capital and share in profits without the responsibility of management.

Line of Credit　An amount of credit granted by a financial institution up to a specified amount for a certain period of time to a borrower.

Liquid Asset　A type of asset that can be easily converted into cash.

Liquidity　The ease with which an individual's or company's assets can be converted to cash without losing their value.

Listing Agreement An agreement between a property owner and a real estate broker that authorizes the broker to attempt to sell or lease the property at a specified price and terms in return for a commission or other compensation.

Loan An amount of money that is borrowed and usually repaid with interest.

Loan Application A document that presents a borrower's income, debt, and other obligations to determine credit worthiness, as well as some basic information on the target property.

Loan Application Fee A fee lenders charge to cover expenses relating to reviewing a loan application.

Loan Commitment An agreement by a lender or other financial institution to make or ensure a loan for the specified amount and terms.

Loan Officer An official representative of a lending institution who is authorized to act on behalf of the lender within specified limits.

Loan Origination The process of obtaining and arranging new loans.

Loan Origination Fee A fee lenders charge to cover the costs related to arranging the loan.

Loan Servicing Process a lending institution goes through for all loans it manages. This involves processing payments, sending statements, managing the escrow/impound account, providing collection services on delinquent loans, ensuring that insurance and property taxes are made on the property, handling pay-offs and assumptions, as well as various other services.

Loan Term The time, usually expressed in years, that a lender sets in which a buyer must pay a mortgage.

Loan-to-Value (LTV) Ratio of the amount of the loan compared to the appraised value or sales price.

Lock-Box Structure Arrangement in which the payments are sent directly from the tenant or borrower to the trustee.

Lock-In A commitment from a lender to a borrower to guarantee a given interest rate for a limited amount of time.

Lock-In Period The period of time during which the borrower is guaranteed a specified interest rate.

Lockout The period of time during which a loan may not be paid off early.

Long-Term Lease A rental agreement that will last at least three years from initial signing to the date of expiration or renewal.

Loss Severity The percentage of lost principal when a loan is foreclosed.

Lot One of several contiguous parcels of a larger piece of land.

Low-Documentation Loan A mortgage that requires only a basic verification of income and assets.

Low-Rise A building that involves fewer than four stories above the ground level.

Lump-Sum Contract A type of construction contract that requires the general contractor to complete a building project for a fixed cost that is usually established beforehand by competitive bidding.

Magic Page A story of projected growth that describes how a new REIT will achieve its future plans for funds from operations or funds available for distribution.

Maintenance Fee The charge to homeowners' association members each month for the repair and maintenance of common areas.

Maker One who issues a promissory note and commits to paying the note when it is due.

Margin A percentage that is added to the index and fixed for the mortgage term.

Mark to Market The act of

changing the original investment cost or value of a property or portfolio to the level of the current estimated market value.

Market Capitalization A measurement of a company's value that is calculated by multiplying the current share price by the current number of shares outstanding.

Market Rental Rates Rental income that a landlord could most likely ask for a property in the open market, indicated by the current rents for comparable spaces.

Market Study A forecast of the demand for a certain type of real estate project in the future that includes an estimate of the square footage that could be absorbed and the rents that could be charged.

Market Value Price a property would sell for at a particular point in time in a competitive market.

Marketable Title A title that is free of encumbrances and can be marketed immediately to a willing purchaser.

Master Lease The primary lease that controls other subsequent leases and may cover more property than all subsequent leases combined.

Master Servicer An entity that acts on behalf of a trustee for security holders' benefit in collecting funds from a borrower, advancing funds in the event of delinquencies and, in the event of default, taking a property through foreclosure.

Maturity Date The date at which the total principal balance of a loan is due.

Mechanic's Lien A claim created for securing payment priority for the price and value of work performed and materials furnished in constructing, repairing, or improving a building or other structure.

Meeting Space The space in hotels that is made available to the public to rent for meetings, conferences, or banquets.

Merged Credit Report A report that combines information from the three primary credit-reporting agencies including: Equifax, Experian, and TransUnion.

Metes and Bounds The surveyed boundary lines of a piece of land described by listing the compass directions (bounds) and distances (metes) of the boundaries.

Mezzanine Financing A financing position somewhere between equity and debt, meaning that there are higher-priority debts above and equity below.

Mid-Rise Usually, a building which shows four to eight stories above ground level. In a business district, buildings up to 25 stories may also be included.

Mixed-Use Term referring to space within a building or project which can be used for more than one activity.

Modern Portfolio Theory (MPT) An approach of quantifying risk and return in an asset portfolio which emphasizes the portfolio rather than the individual assets and how the assets perform in relation to each other.

Modification An adjustment in the terms of a loan agreement.

Modified Annual Percentage Rate (APR) Index of the cost of a loan based on the standard APR but adjusted for the amount of time the borrower expects to hold the loan.

Monthly Association Dues A payment due each month to a homeowners' association for expenses relating to maintenance and community operations.

Mortgage Amount of money borrowed to purchase a property using that property as collateral.

Mortgage Acceleration Clause A provision enabling a lender to require that the rest of the loan balance is paid in a lump sum under certain circumstances.

Mortgage Banker A financial institution that provides home loans using its own resources, often selling them to investors such as insurance companies or Fannie Mae.

Mortgage Broker An individual who matches prospective borrowers with lenders that the broker is approved to deal with.

Mortgage Broker Business A company that matches prospective borrowers with lenders that the broker is approved to deal with.

Mortgage Constant A figure comparing an amortizing mortgage payment to the outstanding mortgage balance.

Mortgage Insurance (MI) Policy, required by lenders on some loans, that covers the lender against certain losses that are incurred as a result of a default on a home loan.

Mortgage Insurance Premium (MIP) The amount charged for mortgage insurance, either to a government agency or to a private MI company.

Mortgage Interest Deduction The tax write-off that the IRS allows most homeowners to deduct for annual interest payments made on real estate loans.

Mortgage Life and Disability Insurance A type of term life insurance borrowers often purchase to cover debt that is left when the borrower dies or becomes too disabled to make the mortgage payments.

Mortgagee The financial institution that lends money to the borrower.

Mortgagor The person who requests to borrow money to purchase a property.

Multi-Dwelling Units A set of properties that provide separate housing areas for more than one family but only require a single mortgage.

Multiple Listing Service A service that lists real estate offered for sale by a particular real estate agent that can be shown or sold by other real estate agents within a certain area.

National Association of Real Estate Investment Trusts (NAREIT) The national, non-profit trade organization that represents the real estate investment trust industry.

National Council of Real Estate Investment Fiduciaries (NCREIF) A group of real estate professionals who serve on committees; sponsor research articles, seminars and symposiums; and produce the NCREIF Property Index.

NCREIF Property Index (NPI) A quarterly and yearly report presenting income and appreciation components.

Negative Amortization An event that occurs when the deferred interest on an ARM is added, and the balance increases instead of decreases.

Net Asset Value (NAV) The total value of an asset or property minus leveraging or joint venture interests.

Net Asset Value Per Share Total value of a REIT's current assets divided by outstanding shares.

Net Assets The total value of assets minus total liabilities based on market value.

Net Cash Flow The total income generated by an investment property after expenses have been subtracted.

Net Investment in Real Estate Gross investment in properties minus the outstanding balance of debt.

Net Investment Income The income or loss of a portfolio or business minus all expenses, including portfolio and asset management fees, but before gains and losses on investments are considered.

Net Operating Income (NOI) The pre-tax figure of gross revenue minus operating expenses and an allowance for expected vacancy.

Net Present Value (NPV) The sum of the total current value of incremental future cash flows plus the current value of estimated sales proceeds.

Net Purchase Price The gross purchase price minus any associated financed debt.

Net Real Estate Investment Value The total market value of all real estate minus property-level debt.

Net Returns The returns paid to investors minus fees to advisers or managers.

Net Sales Proceeds The income from the sale of an asset, or part of an asset, minus brokerage commissions, closing costs, and market expenses.

Net Square Footage The total space required for a task or staff position.

Net Worth The worth of an individual or company figured on the basis of a difference between all assets and liabilities.

No-Cash-Out Refinance Sometimes referred to as a Rate and Term Refinance. A refinancing transaction that is intended only to cover the balance due on the current loan and any costs associated with obtaining the new mortgage.

No-Cost Loan A loan for which there are no costs associated with the loan that are charged by the lender, but with a slightly higher interest rate.

No-Documentation Loan A type of loan application that requires no income or asset verification, usually granted based on strong credit with a large down payment.

Nominal Yield The yield investors receive before it is adjusted for fees, inflation, or risk.

Non-Assumption Clause A provision in a loan agreement that prohibits transferring a mortgage to another borrower without approval from the lender.

Non-Compete Clause A provision in a lease agreement that specifies that the tenant's business is the only one that may operate in the property in question, thereby preventing a competitor moving in next door.

Non-Conforming Loan Any loan that is too large or does not meet certain qualifications to be purchased by Fannie Mae or Freddie Mac.

Non-Discretionary Funds The funds that are allocated to an investment manager who must have approval from the investor for each transaction.

Non-Investment-Grade CMBS Also referred to as High-Yield CMBS. Commercial mortgage-backed securities that have ratings of BB or B.

Non-Liquid Asset A type of asset that is not turned into cash very easily.

Non-Performing Loan A loan agreement that cannot meet its contractual principal and interest payments.

Non-Recourse Debt A loan that limits the lender's options to collect on the value of the real estate in the event of a default by the borrower.

Nonrecurring Closing Costs Fees that are only paid one time in a given transaction.

Note A legal document requiring a borrower to repay a mortgage at a specified interest rate over a certain period of time.

Note Rate The interest rate that is defined in a mortgage note.

Notice of Default A formal written notification a borrower receives once the borrower is in default stating that legal action may be taken.

Offer A term that describes a specified price or spread to sell whole loans or securities.

One-Year Adjustable-Rate Mortgage An ARM for which the interest rate changes annually, generally based on movements of a published index plus a specified margin.

Open Space A section of land or water that has been dedicated for public or private use or enjoyment.

Open-End Fund A type of commingled fund with an infinite life, always accepting new investor capital and making new investments in property.

Operating Cost Escalation A clause that is intended to adjust rents to account for external standards such as published indexes, negotiated wage levels, or building-related expenses.

Operating Expense The regular costs associated with operating and managing a property.

Opportunistic A phrase that generally describes a strategy of holding investments in under performing and/or under-managed assets with the expectation of increases in cash flow and/or value.

Option A condition in which the buyer pays for the right to purchase a property within a certain period of time without the obligation to buy.

Option ARM Loan A type of mortgage in which the borrower has a variety of payment options each month.

Original Principal Balance Total principal owed on a mortgage before a borrower has made a payment.

Origination Fee Fee most lenders charge for covering of the costs associated with arranging the loan.

Originator A company that underwrites loans for commercial and/or multi-family properties.

Out-Parcel The individual retail sites located within a shopping center.

Overallotment A practice in which the underwriters offer and sell a higher number of shares than they had planned to purchase from the issuer.

Owner Financing A transaction in which the property seller agrees to finance all or part of the amount of the purchase.

Parking Ratio A figure, generally expressed as square footage, that compares a building's total rentable square footage to its total number of parking spaces.

Partial Payment An amount paid that is not large enough to cover the normal monthly payment on a mortgage loan.

Partial Sales The act of selling a real estate interest that is smaller than the whole property.

Partial Taking The appropriating of a portion of an owner's property under the laws of Eminent Domain.

Participating Debt Financing that allows the lender to have participatory rights to equity through increased income and/or residual value over the balance of the loan or original value at the time the loan is funded.

Party in Interest Any party that may hold an interest, including employers, unions, and, sometimes, fiduciaries.

Pass-Through Certificate A document that allows the holder to receive payments of principal and interest from the underlying pool of mortgages.

Payment Cap The maximum amount a monthly payment may increase on an ARM.

Payment Change Date The date on which a new payment amount takes effect on an ARM or GPM, usually in the month directly after the adjustment date.

Payout Ratio The percentage of the primary earnings per share, excluding unusual items, that are paid to common stockholders as cash dividends during the next 12 months.

Pension Liability Full amount of capital that is required to finance vested pension fund benefits.

Percentage Rent The amount of rent that is adjusted based on the percentage of gross sales or revenues the tenant receives.

Per-Diem Interest The interest that is charged or accrued daily.

Performance Bond Bond that a contractor posts to guarantee full performance of a contract in which the proceeds will be used for completing the contract or compensating the owner for loss in the event of nonperformance.

Performance Measurement The process of measuring how well an investor's real estate has performed regarding individual assets, advisers/managers, and portfolios.

Performance Changes each quarter in fund or account values that can be explained by investment income, realized or unrealized appreciation, and the total return to the investors before and after investment management fees.

Performance-Based Fees Fees that advisers or managers receive that are based on returns to investors.

Periodic Payment Cap The highest amount that payments can increase or decrease during a given adjustment period on an ARM.

Periodic Rate Cap The maximum amount that the interest rate can increase or decrease during a given adjustment period on an ARM.

Permanent Loan A long-term property mortgage.

Personal Property Any items belonging to a person that is not real estate.

PITI Principal, Interest, Taxes, Insurance The items that are included in the monthly payment to the lender for an impounded loan, as well as mortgage insurance.

PITI Reserves The amount in cash that a borrower must readily have after the down payment and all closing costs are paid when purchasing a home.

Plan Assets The assets included in a pension plan.

Plan Sponsor The party that is responsible for administering an employee benefit plan.

Planned Unit Development (PUD) A type of ownership where individuals actually own the building or unit they live in, but common areas are owned jointly with the other members of the development or association. Contrast with condominium, where an individual actually owns the airspace of his unit, but the buildings and common areas are owned jointly with the others in the development or association.

Plat A chart or map of a certain area showing the boundaries of individual lots, streets, and easements.

Pledged Account Mortgage (PAM) A loan tied to a pledged savings account for which the fund and earned interest are used to gradually reduce mortgage payments.

Point Also referred to as a Discount Point. A fee a lender charges to provide a lower interest rate, equal to 1 percent of the amount of the loan.

Portfolio Management A process that involves formulating, modifying, and implementing a real estate investment strategy according to an investor's investment objectives.

Portfolio Turnover Amount of time averaged from the time an investment is funded until it is repaid or sold.

Power of Attorney A legal document that gives someone the authority to act on behalf of another party.

Power of Sale Clause included in a mortgage or deed of trust that provides the mortgagee (or trustee) with the right and power to advertise and sell the property at public auction if the borrower is in default.

Pre-Approval Complete analysis a lender makes regarding a potential borrower's ability to pay for a home as well as a confirmation of the proposed amount to be borrowed.

Pre-Approval Letter The letter a lender presents that states the amount of money they are willing to lend a potential buyer.

Preferred Shares Certain stocks that have a prior distributions claim up to a defined amount before the common shareholders may receive anything.

Pre-Leased A certain amount of space in a proposed building that must be leased before construction may begin or a certificate of occupancy may be issued.

Prepaid Expenses The amount of money that is paid before it is due, including taxes, insurance, and/or assessments.

Prepaid Fees The charges that a borrower must pay in advance regarding certain recurring items, such as interest, property taxes, hazard insurance, and PMI, if applicable.

Prepaid Interest Amount of interest paid before its due date.

Prepayment Money that is paid to reduce the principal balance of a loan before the date it is due.

Prepayment Penalty A penalty that may be charged to the borrower when he pays off a loan before the planned maturity date.

Prepayment Rights The right a borrower is given to pay the total principal balance before the maturity date free of penalty.

Prequalification The initial assessment by a lender of a potential borrower's ability to pay

for a home as well as an estimate of how much the lender is willing to supply to the buyer.

Price-to-Earnings Ratio The comparison that is derived by dividing the current share price by the sum of the primary earnings per share from continuing operations over the past year.

Primary Issuance The preliminary financing of an issuer.

Prime Rate The best interest rate reserved for a bank's preferred customers.

Prime Space The first-generation space that is available for lease.

Prime Tenant The largest or highest-earning tenant in a building or shopping center.

Principal The amount of money originally borrowed in a mortgage, before interest is included and with any payments subtracted.

Principal Balance The total current balance of mortgage principal not including interest.

Principal Paid over Life of Loan The final total of scheduled payments to the principal that the lender calculates to equal the face amount of the loan.

Principal Payments The lender's return of invested capital.

Principle of Conformity The concept that a property will probably increase in value if its size, age, condition, and style are similar to other properties in the immediate area.

Private Debt Mortgages or other liabilities for which an individual is responsible.

Private Equity A real estate investment that has been acquired by a noncommercial entity.

Private Mortgage Insurance (PMI) A type of policy that a lender requires when the borrower's down payment or home equity percentage is under 20 percent of the value of the property.

Private Placement The sale of a security in a way that renders it exempt from the registration rules and requirements of the SEC.

Private REIT A real estate investment company that is structured as a real estate investment trust that places and holds shares privately rather than publicly.

Pro Rata The proportionate amount of expenses per tenant for the property's maintenance and operation.

Processing Fee A fee some lenders charge for gathering the information necessary to process the loan.

Production Acres The portion of land that can be used directly in agriculture or timber activities to generate income, but not areas used for such things as machinery storage or support.

Prohibited Transaction Certain transactions that may not be performed between a pension plan and a party in interest, such as the following: the sale, exchange or lease of any property; a loan or other grant of credit; and furnishing goods or services.

Promissory Note A written agreement to repay the specific amount over a certain period of time.

Property Tax The tax that must be paid on private property.

Prudent Man Rule The standard to which ERISA holds a fiduciary accountable.

Public Auction An announced public meeting held at a specified location for the purpose of selling property to repay a mortgage in default.

Public Debt Mortgages or other liabilities for which a commercial entity is responsible.

Public Equity A real estate investment that has been acquired by REITs and other publicly traded real estate operating companies.

Punch List An itemized list that documents incomplete or unsatisfactory items after the contractor has declared the space to be mostly complete.

Purchase Agreement The written contract the buyer and seller both sign defining the terms and conditions under which a property is sold.

Purchase Money Transaction A transaction in which property is acquired through the exchange of money or something of equivalent value.

Purchase-Money Mortgage (PMM) A mortgage obtained by a borrower that serves as partial payment for a property.

Qualified Plan Any employee benefit plan that the IRS has approved as a tax-exempt plan.

Qualifying Ratio The measurement a lender uses to determine how much they are willing to lend to a potential buyer.

Quitclaim Deed A written document that releases a party from any interest they may have in a property.

Rate Cap The highest interest rate allowed on a monthly payment during an adjustment period of an ARM.

Rate Lock The commitment of a lender to a borrower that guarantees a certain interest rate for a specific amount of time.

Rate-Improvement Mortgage A loan that includes a clause that entitles a borrower to a one-time-only cut in the interest rate without having to refinance.

Rating Agencies Independent firms that are engaged to rate securities' creditworthiness on behalf of investors.

Rating A figure that represents the credit quality or creditworthiness of securities.

Raw Land A piece of property that has not been developed and remains in its natural state.

Raw Space Shell space in a building that has not yet been developed.

Real Estate Agent An individual who is licensed to negotiate and transact the real estate sales.

Real Estate Fundamentals The factors that drive the value of property.

Real Estate Settlement Procedures Act (RESPA) A legislation for consumer protection that requires lenders to notify borrowers regarding closing costs in advance.

Real Property Land and anything else of a permanent nature that is affixed to the land.

Real Rate of Return The yield given to investors minus an inflationary factor.

Realtor A real estate agent or broker who is an active member of a local real estate board affiliated with the National Association of Realtors.

Recapture The act of the IRS recovering the tax benefit of a deduction or a credit that a taxpayer has previously taken in error.

Recorder A public official who records transactions that affect real estate in the area.

Recording The documentation that the registrar's office keeps of the details of properly executed legal documents.

Recording Fee A fee real estate agents charge for moving the sale of a piece of property into the public record.

Recourse The option a lender has for recovering losses against the personal assets of a secondary party who is also liable for a debt that is in default.

Red Herring An early prospectus that is distributed to prospective investors that includes a note in red ink on the cover stating that the SEC-approved registration statement is not yet in effect.

Refinance Transaction The act of paying off an existing loan using the funding gained from a new loan that uses the same property as security.

Regional Diversification Boundaries that are defined based on geography or economic lines.

Registration Statement The set of forms that are filed with the SEC (or the appropriate state agency) regarding a proposed offering of new securities or the listing of outstanding securities on a national exchange.

Regulation Z A federal legislation under the Truth in Lending Act that requires lenders to advise the borrower in writing of all costs that are associated with the credit portion of a financial transaction.

Rehab Short for Rehabilitation. Refers to an extensive renovation intended to extend the life of a building or project.

Rehabilitation Mortgage A loan meant to fund the repairing and improving of a resale home or building.

Real Estate Investment Trust (REIT) A trust corporation that combines the capital of several investors for the purpose of acquiring or providing funding for real estate.

Remaining Balance The amount of the principal on a home loan that has not yet been paid.

Remaining Term The original term of the loan after the number of payments made has been subtracted.

Real Estate Mortgage Investment Conduit (REMIC) An investment vehicle that is designed to hold a pool of mortgages solely to issue multiple classes of mortgage-backed securities in a way that avoids doubled corporate tax.

Renewal Option Clause in a lease agreement that allows a tenant to extend the term of a lease.

Renewal Probability The average percentage of a building's tenants who are expected to renew terms at market rental rates upon the lease expiration.

Rent Commencement Date The date at which a tenant is to begin paying rent.

Rent Loss Insurance A policy that covers loss of rent or rental value for a landlord due to any condition that renders the leased premises inhabitable, thereby excusing the tenant from paying rent.

Rent The fee paid for the occupancy and/or use of any rental property or equipment.

Rentable/Usable Ratio A total rentable area in a building divided by the area available for use.

Rental Concession See: Concessions.

Rental Growth Rate The projected trend of market rental rates over a particular period of analysis.

Rent-Up Period The period of time following completion of a new building when tenants are actively being sought and the project is stabilizing.

Real Estate Owned (REO) Real estate that a savings institution owns as a result of foreclosure on borrowers in default.

Repayment Plan Agreement made to repay late installments or advances.

Replacement Cost Projected cost by current standards of constructing a building equivalent to the building being appraised.

Replacement Reserve Fund Money that is set aside for replacing of common property in a condominium, PUD, or cooperative project.

Request for Proposal (RFP) Formal request that invites investment managers to submit information regarding investment strategies, historical investment performance, current investment opportunities, investment management fees, and other pension fund client relationships used by their firm.

Rescission The legal withdrawing of a contract or consent from the parties involved.

Reserve Account An account that must be funded by the borrower to protect the lender.

Resolution Trust Corp. (RTC) The congressional corporation established for the purpose of containing, managing, and selling failed financial institutions, thereby recovering taxpayer funds.

Retail Investor Investor who sells interests directly to consumers.

Retention Rate The percentage of trailing year's earnings that have been dispersed into the company again. It is calculated as 100 minus the trailing 12-month payout ratio.

Return on Assets The measurement of the ability to produce net profits efficiently by making use of assets.

Return on Equity The measurement of the return on the investment in a business or property.

Return on Investments Percentage of money gained as a result of certain investments.

Reverse Mortgage See: Home Equity Conversion Mortgage.

Reversion Capitalization Rate The capitalization rate that is used to derive reversion value.

Reversion Value A benefit that an investor expects to receive as a lump sum at the end of an investment.

Revolving Debt A credit arrangement that enables a customer to borrow against a predetermined line of credit when purchasing goods and services.

Revenue per Available Room (RevPAR) The total room revenue for a particular period divided by the average number of rooms available in a hospitality facility.

Right of Ingress or Egress The option to enter or to leave the premises in question.

Right of Survivorship The option that survivors have to take on the interest of a deceased joint tenant.

Right to Rescission A legal provision that enables borrowers to cancel certain loan types within three days after they sign.

Risk Management A logical approach to analyzing and defining insurable and non-insurable risks while evaluating the availability and costs of purchasing third-party insurance.

Risk-Adjusted Rate of Return A percentage that is used to identify investment options that are expected to deliver a positive premium despite their volatility.

Road Show A tour of the executives of a company that is planning to go public, during which the executives travel to a variety of cities to make presentations to underwriters and analysts regarding their company and IPO.

Roll-Over Risk The possibility that tenants will not renew their lease.

Sale-Leaseback Arrangement in which a seller deeds a property, or part of it, to a buyer in exchange for money or the equivalent, then leases the property from the new owner.

Sales Comparison Value A value that is calculated by comparing the appraised property to similar properties in the area that have been recently sold.

Sales Contract Agreement both the buyer and seller sign defining the terms of a property sale.

Second Mortgage Secondary loan obtained on a piece of property.

Secondary Market A market in which existing mortgages are bought and sold as part of a mortgages pool.

Secondary (Follow-On) Offering An offering of stock made by a company that is already public.

Second-Generation or Secondary Space Space that has been occupied before and becomes available for lease again, either by the landlord or as a sublease.

Secured Loan A loan that is secured by some sort of collateral.

Securities and Exchange Commission (SEC) The federal agency that oversees the issuing and exchanging of public securities.

Securitization The act of converting a non-liquid asset into a tradable form.

Security The property or other asset that will serve as a loan's collateral.

Security Deposit An amount of money a tenant gives to a landlord to secure the performance of terms in a lease agreement.

Seisen (Seizen) The ownership of real property under a claim of freehold estate.

Self-Administered REIT A REIT in which the management are employees of the REIT or similar entity.

Self-Managed REIT See: Self-Administered REIT.

Seller Carry-Back An arrangement in which the seller provides the financing to purchase a home.

Seller Financing A type of funding in which the borrower may use part of the equity in the property to finance the purchase.

Senior Classes The security classes who have the highest priority for receiving payments from the underlying mortgage loans.

Separate Account A relationship in which a single pension plan sponsor is used to retain an investment manager or adviser under a stated investment policy exclusively for that sponsor.

Servicer An organization that collects principal and interest payments from borrowers and manages borrowers' escrow accounts on behalf of a trustee.

Servicing The process of collecting mortgage payments from borrowers as well as related responsibilities.

Setback The distance required from a given reference point before a structure can be built.

Settlement or Closing Fees Fees that the escrow agent receives for carrying out the written instructions in the agreement between borrower and lender and/or buyer and seller.

Settlement Statement See: HUD-1 Settlement Statement.

Shared-Appreciation Mortgage A loan that enables a lender or other party to share in the profits of the borrower when the borrower sells the home.

Shared-Equity Transaction A transaction in which two people purchase a property, one as a residence and the other as an investment.

Shares Outstanding The number of shares of outstanding common stock minus the treasury shares.

Site Analysis A determination of how suitable a specific parcel of land is for a particular use.

Site Development The implementation of all improvements that are needed for a site before construction may begin.

Site Plan A detailed description and map of the location of improvements to a parcel.

Slab The flat, exposed surface that is laid over the structural support beams to form the building's floor(s).

Social Investing A strategy in which investments are driven in partially or completely by social or non-real estate objectives.

Soft Cost Part of an equity investment, aside from literal cost of the improvements, that could be tax-deductible in the first year.

Space Plan Chart or map of space requirements for a tenant that includes wall/door locations, room sizes, and even furniture layouts.

Special Assessment Certain charges that are levied against real estates for public improvements to benefit the property in question.

Special Servicer Company that is hired to collect on mortgages that are either delinquent or in default.

Specified Investing A strategy of investment in individually specified properties, portfolios, or commingled funds are fully or partially detailed prior to the commitment of investor capital.

Speculative Space Any space in a rental property that has not been leased prior to construction on a new building begins.

Stabilized Net Operating Income Expected income minus expenses that reflect relatively stable operations.

Stabilized Occupancy The best projected range of long-term occupancy that a piece of rental property will achieve after existing in the open market for a reasonable period of time with terms and conditions that are comparable to similar offerings.

Step-Rate Mortgage A loan that allows for a gradual interest rate increase during the first few years of the loan.

Step-Up Lease (Graded Lease) A lease agreement that specifies certain increases in rent at certain intervals during the complete term of the lease.

Straight Lease (Flat Lease) A lease agreement that specifies an amount of rent that should be paid regularly during the complete term of the lease.

Strip Center Any shopping area that is made up of a row of stores but is not large enough to be anchored by a grocery store.

Subcontractor A contractor who has been hired by the general contractor, often specializing in a certain required task for the construction project.

Subdivision The most common type of housing development created by dividing a larger tract of land into individual lots for sale or lease.

Sublessee A person or business that holds the rights of use and occupancy under a lease contract with the original lessee, who still retains primary responsibility for the lease obligations.

Subordinate Financing Any loan with a priority lower than loans that were obtained beforehand.

Subordinate Loan Second or third mortgage obtained with the same property being used as collateral.

Subordinated Classes Classes that have the lowest priority of receiving payments from underlying mortgage loans.

Subordination Act of sharing credit loss risk at varying rates among two or more classes of securities.

Subsequent Rate Adjustments The interest rate for ARMs that adjusts at regular intervals, sometimes differing from the duration period of the initial interest rate.

Subsequent Rate Cap The maximum amount the interest rate may increase at each regularly scheduled interest rate adjustment date on an ARM.

Super Jumbo Mortgage A loan that is over $650,000 for some lenders or $1,000,000 for others.

Surety A person who willingly binds himself to the debt or obligation of another party.

Surface Rights A right or easement that is usually granted with mineral rights that enables the holder to drill through the surface.

Survey A document or analysis containing the precise measurements of a piece of property as performed by a licensed surveyor.

Sweat Equity The non-cash improvements in value that an owner adds to a piece of property.

Synthetic Lease A transaction that is considered to be a lease by accounting standards but a loan by tax standards.

Taking Similar to condemning, or any other interference with rights to private property, but a physical seizure or appropriation is not required.

Tax Base The determined value of all property that lies within the jurisdiction of the taxing authority.

Tax Lien Type of lien placed against a property if the owner has not paid property or personal taxes.

Tax Roll A record that contains the descriptions of all land parcels and their owners that is located within the county.

Tax Service Fee A fee that is charged for the purpose of setting up monitoring of the borrower's property tax payments by a third party.

Teaser Rate A small, short-term interest rate offered on a mortgage in order to convince the potential borrower to apply.

Tenancy by the Entirety A form of ownership held by spouses in which they both hold title to the entire property with right of survivorship.

Tenancy in Common A type of ownership held by two or more owners in an undivided interest in the property with no right of survivorship.

Tenant (Lessee) Party who rents a piece of real estate from another by way of a lease agreement.

Tenant at Will A person who possesses a piece of real estate with the owner's permission.

Tenant Improvement (TI) Allowance The specified amount of money that the landlord contributes toward tenant improvements.

Tenant Improvement (TI) The upgrades or repairs that are made to the leased premises by or for a tenant.

Tenant Mix The quality of the income stream for a property.

Term Length that a loan lasts or is expected to last before it is repaid.

Third-Party Origination A process in which another party is used by the lender to originate, process, underwrite, close, fund, or package the mortgages it expects to deliver to the secondary mortgage market.

Timeshare A form of ownership involving purchasing a specific period of time or percentage of interest in a vacation property.

Time-Weighted Average Annual Rate of Return The regular yearly return over several years that would have the same return value as combining the actual annual returns for each year in the series.

Title The legal written document that provides someone ownership in a piece of real estate.

Title Company A business that determines that a property title is clear and that provides title insurance.

Title Exam An analysis of the public records in order to confirm that the seller is the legal owner, and there are no encumbrances on the property.

Title Insurance A type of policy that is issued to both lenders and buyers to cover loss due to property ownership disputes that may arise at a later date.

Title Insurance Binder A written promise from the title insurance company to insure the title to the property, based on the conditions and exclusions shown in the binder.

Title Risk The potential impediments in transferring a title from one party to another.

Title Search Process of analyzing all transactions existing in the public record in order to determine whether any title defects could interfere with the clear transfer of property ownership.

Total Acres The complete amount of land area that is contained within a real estate investment.

Total Assets The final amount of all gross investments, cash and equivalents, receivables, and other assets as they are presented on the balance sheet.

Total Commitment The complete funding amount that is promised once all specified conditions have been met.

Total Expense Ratio The comparison of monthly debt obligations to gross monthly income.

Total Inventory The total amount of square footage commanded by property within a geographical area.

Total Lender Fees Charges that the lender requires for obtaining the loan, aside from other fees associated with the transfer of a property.

Total Loan Amount The basic amount of the loan plus any additional financed closing costs.

Total Monthly Housing Costs The amount that must be paid each month to cover principal, interest, property taxes, PMI, and/or either hazard insurance or homeowners' association dues.

Total of All Payments The total cost of the loan after figuring the sum of all monthly interest payments.

Total Principal Balance The sum of all debt, including the original loan amount adjusted for subsequent payments and any unpaid items that may be included in the principal balance by the mortgage note or by law.

Total Retail Area The total floor area of a retail center that is currently leased or available for lease.

Total Return The final amount of income and appreciation returns per quarter.

Townhouse An attached home that is not considered to be a condominium.

Trade Fixtures Any personal property that is attached to a structure and used in the business but is removable once the lease is terminated.

Trading Down The act of purchasing a property that is less expensive than the one currently owned.

Trading Up The act of purchasing a property that is more expensive than the one currently owned.

Tranche A class of securities that may or may not be rated.

TransUnion Corporation One of the primary credit-reporting bureaus.

Transfer of Ownership Any process in which a property changes hands from one owner to another.

Transfer Tax An amount specified by state or local authorities when ownership in a piece of property changes hands.

Treasury Index A measurement that is used to derive interest rate changes for ARMs.

Triple Net Lease A lease that requires the tenant to pay all property expenses on top of the rental payments.

Trustee A fiduciary who oversees property or funds on behalf of another party.

Truth-in-Lending The federal legislation requiring lenders to fully disclose the terms and conditions of a mortgage in writing.

TurnKey Project A project in which all components are within a single supplier's responsibility.

Two- to Four-Family Property A structure that provides living space for two to four families while ownership is held in a single deed.

Two-Step Mortgage An ARM with two different interest rates: one for the loan's first five or seven years and another for the remainder of the loan term.

Under Construction The time period that exists after a building's construction has started but before a certificate of occupancy has been presented.

Under Contract The period of time during which a buyer's offer to purchase a property has been accepted, and the buyer is able to finalize financing arrangements without the concern of the seller making a deal with another buyer.

Underwriter A company, usually an investment banking firm, that is involved in a guarantee that an entire issue of stocks or bonds will be purchased.

Underwriters' Knot An approved knot according to code that may be tied at the end of an electrical cord to prevent the wires from being pulled away from their connection to each other or to electrical terminals.

Underwriting The process during which lenders analyze the risks a particular borrower presents and set appropriate conditions for the loan.

Underwriting Fee A fee that mortgage lenders charge for verifying the information on the loan application and making a final decision on approving the loan.

Unencumbered A term that refers to property free of liens or other encumbrances.

Unimproved Land See: Raw Land.

Unrated Classes Usually the lowest classes of securities.

Unrecorded Deed A deed that transfers right of ownership from one owner to another without being officially documented.

Umbrella Partnership Real Estate Investment Trust (UPREIT) An organizational structure in which a REIT's assets are owned by a holding company for tax reasons.

Usable Square Footage The total area that is included within the exterior walls of the tenant's space.

Use The particular purpose for which a property is intended to be employed.

VA Loan A mortgage through the VA program in which a down payment is not necessarily required.

Vacancy Factor The percentage of gross revenue that pro-forma income statements expect to be lost due to vacancies.

Vacancy Rate The percentage of space that is available to rent.

Vacant Space Existing rental space that is presently being marketed for lease minus space that is available for sublease.

Value-Added Phrase advisers and managers generally use to describe investments in underperforming and/or under-managed assets.

Variable Rate Mortgage (VRM) A loan in which the interest rate changes according to fluctuations in particular indexes.

Variable Rate Also called adjustable rate. The interest rate on a loan that varies over the term of the loan according to a predetermined index.

Variance A permission that enables a property owner to work around a zoning ordinance's literal requirements which cause a unique hardship due to special circumstances.

Verification of Deposit (VOD) The confirmation statement a borrower's bank may be asked to sign in order to verify the borrower's account balances and history.

Verification of Employment (VOE) The confirmation statement a borrower's employer may be asked to sign in order to verify the borrower's position and salary.

Vested Having the right to draw on a portion or on all of a pension or other retirement fund.

Veterans Affairs (VA) A federal government agency that assists veterans in purchasing a home without a down payment.

Virtual Storefront A retail business presence on the Internet.

Waiting Period The period of time between initially filing a registration statement and the date it becomes effective.

Warehouse Fee A closing cost fee that represents the lender's expense of temporarily holding a borrower's loan before it is sold on the secondary mortgage market.

Weighted-Average Coupon The average, using the balance of each mortgage as the weighting factor, of the gross interest rates of the mortgages underlying a pool as of the date of issue.

Weighted-Average Equity The part of the equation that is used to calculate investment-level income, appreciation, and total returns on a quarter-by-quarter basis.

Weighted-Average Rental Rates The average ratio of unequal rental rates across two or more buildings in a market.

Working Drawings The detailed blueprints for a construction project that comprise the contractual documents which describe the exact manner in which a project is to be built.

Workout Strategy in which a borrower negotiates with a lender to attempt to restructure the borrower's debt rather than go through the foreclosure proceedings.

Wraparound Mortgage Loan obtained by a buyer to use for the remaining balance on the seller's first mortgage, as well as an additional amount requested by the seller.

Write-Down A procedure used in accounting when an asset's book value is adjusted downward to reflect current market value more accurately.

Write-Off A procedure used in accounting when an asset is determined to be uncollectible and is therefore considered to be a loss.

Yield Maintenance Premium A penalty the borrower must pay in order to make investors whole in the event of early repayment of principal.

Yield Spread The difference in income derived from a commercial mortgage and from a benchmark value.

Yield The actual return on an investment, usually paid in dividends or interest.

Zoning Ordinance The regulations and laws that control the use or improvement of land in a particular area or zone.

Zoning The act of dividing a city or town into particular areas and applying laws and regulations regarding the architectural design, structure, and intended uses of buildings within those areas.

Index

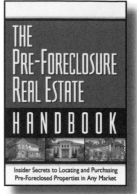
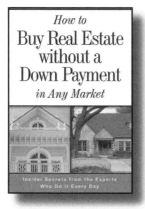
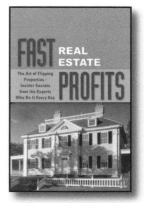

MORE GREAT TITLES FROM ATLANTIC PUBLISHING

THE COMPLETE GUIDE TO INVESTING IN REAL ESTATE TAX LIENS & DEEDS: HOW TO EARN HIGH RATES OF RETURN—SAFELY

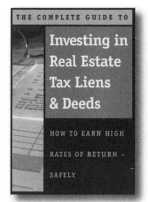

Tax lien certificates and deeds are not purchased through a broker; you purchase these property tax liens directly from the state or county government (depending on the state). This type of investment was created by state law, and state law protects you as the investor. Investing in tax liens and deeds can be very rewarding. Tax liens can be tax deferred or even tax-free. You can purchase them in your self-directed IRA. Interest rates vary but average between 4% and 18%. The interest rates are fixed by local governments, essentially a government-guaranteed loan. This sounds great, but what is the catch? There really is none, except you must know what you are doing! This groundbreaking book will provide everything you need to know to get you started on generating high-investment returns with low risk, from start to finish. **320 Pages • Item # CGI-02 • $21.95**

THE SECOND HOMEOWNER'S HANDBOOK: A COMPLETE GUIDE FOR VACATION, INCOME, RETIREMENT, AND INVESTMENT

There is no better time than now to buy that second home you've been thinking about for getaways, vacations, investment, or retirement. Low interest rates, tax savings, rising appreciation, and effortless financing make it simple to profit from a second home. This book explains how to invest profitably in a vacation or future retirement home. Your second home can be for living, to re-sell, or even rent. This comprehensive guide presents proven tactics to make your second home a smooth and profitable transaction. You will learn precisely what to look for in a real estate investment, buying prospects, and how to make your current home groundwork for potential real estate investments, how to find the best opportunities, negotiating, financing, budgets, credit reports and more. **288 Pages • Item # SHO-02 • $21.95**

PRIVATE MORTGAGE INVESTING: HOW TO EARN 12% OR MORE ON YOUR SAVINGS, INVESTMENTS, IRA ACCOUNTS AND PERSONAL EQUITY: A COMPLETE RESOURCE GUIDE WITH 100s OF HINTS, TIPS & SECRETS FROM EXPERTS WHO DO IT EVERY DAY

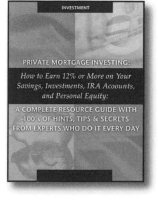

This book provides detailed information on how to put money to work in a relatively safe private mortgage investment with a high return of 12 to 15 percent (or more) in most cases. Private mortgages have grown into a multi-billion-dollar industry. This market allows investors to earn substantially higher yields—while offering the security of real property to back the loan. **400 Pages • Item # PMI-01 • $29.95**

To order call 1-800-814-1132 or visit www.atlantic-pub.com

MORE GREAT TITLES FROM ATLANTIC PUBLISHING

THE REAL ESTATE INVESTOR'S HANDBOOK: THE COMPLETE GUIDE FOR THE INDIVIDUAL INVESTOR

This book is a must-have for beginning investors, real estate veterans, commercial brokers, sellers, and buyers. This comprehensive step-by-step proven program shows beginners and seasoned veterans alike the ins and outs of real estate investing. This book is a road map to successful investing in real estate. Real estate appreciates at a rate far greater than the rate of inflation, builds equity, provides a steady return on investment, provides cash flow, and can offer substantial tax benefits. This handbook is the resource for novices and pros alike; it will guide you through every step of the process of real estate investing. You will uncover secrets that expert real estate investors use every day. This comprehensive resource contains a wealth of modern tips and strategies for getting started in this very lucrative area.

392 Pages • Item # RIH-02 • $24.95

THE RENTAL PROPERTY MANAGER'S TOOLBOX—A COMPLETE GUIDE INCLUDING PRE-WRITTEN FORMS, AGREEMENTS, LETTERS, AND LEGAL NOTICES: WITH COMPANION CD-ROM

This book and will teach you how to professionally manage your rental property. Maximize your profits and minimize your risks. Learn about advertising, tenants, legal rights, landlord rights, discrimination, vacancies, essential lease clauses, crime prevention, security issues, as well as premises liability, security deposits, handling problems, evictions, maintenance, recordkeeping, and taxes. The CD-ROM contains dozens of forms, sample contracts and more.

384 Pages • Item # RPM-02 • $29.95 with Companion CD-ROM

To order call 1-800-814-1132 or visit www.atlantic-pub.com